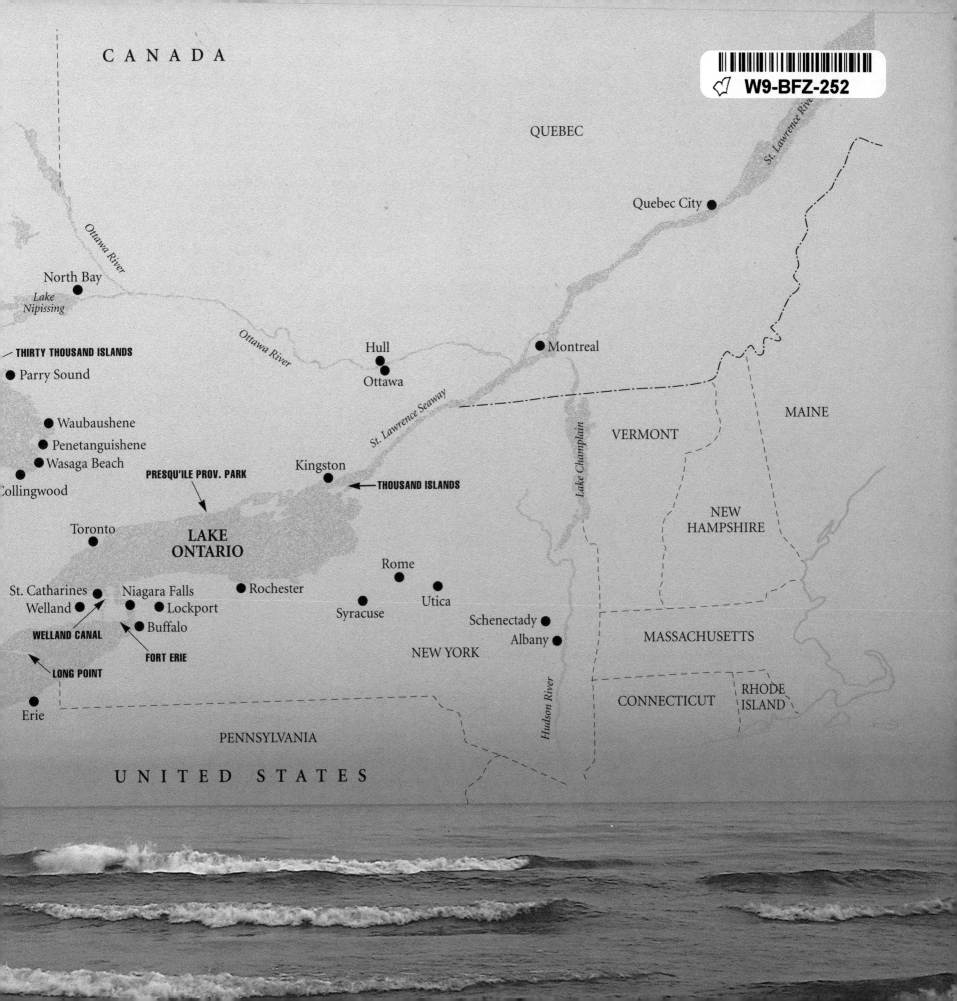

CANADA

QUEBEC

St. Lawrence River

Quebec City

Ottawa River

North Bay

Lake Nipissing

Ottawa River

Hull

Montreal

THIRTY THOUSAND ISLANDS

Parry Sound

St. Lawrence Seaway

MAINE

Waubaushene

VERMONT

Penetanguishene

Lake Champlain

Wasaga Beach

Kingston

PRESQU'ILE PROV. PARK

← **THOUSAND ISLANDS**

NEW HAMPSHIRE

Collingwood

LAKE ONTARIO

Toronto

Rome

St. Catharines

Niagara Falls

Rochester

Welland

Lockport

Utica

Syracuse

Schenectady

MASSACHUSETTS

WELLAND CANAL

Buffalo

FORT ERIE

Albany

NEW YORK

LONG POINT

CONNECTICUT

RHODE ISLAND

Erie

Hudson River

PENNSYLVANIA

U N I T E D   S T A T E S

PIERRE BERTON

THE GREAT LAKES

PHOTOGRAPHS BY ANDRÉ GALLANT

PIERRE BERTON

THE GREAT LAKES

PHOTOGRAPHS BY ANDRÉ GALLANT

Published in 1996 by
Stoddart Publishing Co. Limited
34 Lesmill Road, Toronto, Canada M3B 2T6
Tel. (416) 445-3333   Fax (416) 445-5967

Stoddart Books are available for bulk purchase for sales promotions,
premiums, fundraising, and seminars. For details,
contact the Special Sales Department at the above address.

Canadian Cataloguing in Publication Data
Berton, Pierre, 1920-
The Great Lakes
ISBN 0-7737-2971-2
1. Great Lakes. I. Title
F551.B47 1996   977   C96-930423-4

Printed in Singapore

HALF TITLE: **Sunrise, Blind River, Ontario: Lake Huron**
TITLE PAGE: **Lighthouse, Grand Haven, Michigan: Lake Michigan**
BELOW: **Crowds of bathers, Hanlan's Point, Toronto: Lake Ontario, circa 1912**

CONTENTS

LAKE SUPERIOR

(so called not because of its size

but because of its northwesterly

position) I see as remorseless

and masculine

LAKE HURON,

with its thirty thousand

islands, reminds me of a

fussy maiden aunt.

LAKE MICHIGAN,
half wild to the north,
heavily industrialized
to the south, is an
errant uncle.

LAKE ERIE
is a wilful ingenue of
changeable mood and
false promise.

LAKE ONTARIO

is a complacent child.

LAKE ONTARIO

is a complacent child.

INTRODUCTION

THOSE OF US WHO LIVE AND WORK BESIDE THE GREAT LAKES ACCEPT THEIR magnitude with scarcely a passing thought. We have long since grown used to them and are not awed by their size, as newcomers are, or terrified by their power, as sailors learn to be. We do not see them as the first Europeans saw them, with wide-eyed astonishment: vast inland seas—and, amazingly, fresh. How could such an expanse of water be anything but salt? Champlain, hurtling down the French River by canoe and bursting upon the apparently limitless expanse of Georgian Bay, thought he had arrived on the shores of the great South Sea. But when he dipped his fingers in the water, he found it sweet. It became *La Mer douce*—"the sweet sea"—but a sea, for all that.

They seem to have been here forever, these inland oceans, but actually they are very young. They constitute one of the youngest natural features on the continent, a truth that may surprise those who think of them as ageless. Compared to the Precambrian Shield on whose rim they rest, they are no more than a blink in geological time. If the age of the Shield (two billion years) is represented as a month, then the lakes are no more than three and a half minutes old.

The human species is far older than the lakes. Homo sapiens walked the earth for at least twenty-five millennia before the lakes were formed. There were human beings present when they began to take shape. And so we no longer pretend that Champlain and his young protégé, Etienne Brûlé, "discovered" them. By deleting that word from the lexicon of exploration, we pay homage to the various cultures that have existed beside the lakes for at least thirteen thousand years. Even as the last ice sheet began its long retreat there were people here hunting mastodon and caribou.

These are not the same lakes those aboriginals knew. During the long centuries when the ice was retreating, their shapes were changed many times. Their context has also changed. The original species of fish on which Brûlé and his Hurons must have fed are gone, replaced in part by foreign exotics, many of them dumped in these waters from the bilges of the ocean steamers that can now traverse the entire system. A chemical stew, the by-product of industrial "progress," has transformed waters that once glittered crystal clear in the sunlight. And the great forests that once seemed endless and perpetual have disappeared. Even the stumps have vanished.

Indian Encampment on Lake Huron c. 1845-50, Paul Kane, Art Gallery of Ontario, (detail)

ABOVE: Champlain's first view of Georgian Bay at the mouth of the French River, as it must have looked to the early explorers. OPPOSITE: *Indian Encampment on Lake Huron* **circa 1845–50, by Paul Kane (detail), oil on canvas, Art Gallery of Ontario.**

The lakes provide and the lakes destroy. Some of the treasure torn from the rocks that ring the inland seas lies hidden beneath the waters, lost among the rubble of broken freighters. We have been profligate with our lakes. Shorelines have been filled in, cemented over, and ripped apart to form the cities that sprang up at the river mouths. For centuries the lakes have been the source of incalculable wealth, from furs to hydro power; they sprawl today over the richest corner of the continent; but we are only now coming to understand that we can no longer take them for granted.

No wonder the first explorers thought of these lakes as oceans. Here is one-fifth of the world's fresh water, stored in a series of prehistoric basins. There is enough here to cover the surface of most of western Europe—to drown all of Germany, France, Italy, Spain, Portugal, and the three Benelux countries. With the St. Lawrence the lakes form a water corridor that stretches into the heart of the continent. Think of this: the distance from the western tip of Superior to the Thousand Islands is equal to that from Paris to Bucharest. And you could easily fit the entire United Kingdom into the space that lies between Superior's northern shore and the southern tip of Lake Michigan.

Each inland sea is like a small nation in its infinite variety. Each has its own character, or so it seems to me. I see Superior—so called not because of its size but because of its northwesterly position—as remorseless and masculine. Huron, with its thirty thousand islands, reminds me of a fussy maiden aunt. Michigan, half wild to the north, heavily industrialized to the south, is an errant uncle. Erie is a wilful ingenue of changeable mood and false promise. Ontario is a complacent child.

I will never forget when, on a freezing January day, standing on the rim of Superior where the Canadian Pacific Railway hugs the Precambrian Shield and looking down on its hard and chilly expanse, with chattering teeth I did my best to talk for the television cameras. I was trying to picture a piece of history, to explain what it was like for those troops who were being sent out to the District of Saskatchewan in 1885 to crush Riel and were forced to trudge across this frozen piece of lake between sections of the unfinished rail line. As the wind howled around me and the very cameras froze, I could almost see that line of shadowy figures stumbling westward over the ice.

I first encountered Georgian Bay in 1948 in the form of Wasaga Beach, a teeming anthill of sweating humanity strewn over the white sands that also served, incongruously, as a combined raceway and parking lot for thousands of tourist automobiles. The tourists are still there, roasting in the summer sun, but happily the motorcars have been banned at last from this strip of cottage country.

I first saw Lake Michigan from Chicago and marvelled at a city so far-sighted that it had managed to save its lakefront from the entrepreneurs and the developers. As far back as 1836 it was set aside as public ground. This is one of the few lake cities where you can walk along a greensward beside the water, unobstructed by hotels or factories. Toronto is only now waking up to that possibility and trying, not without difficulty, to make amends.

Erie is my favourite lake because of the three long spits that stretch like fingers into the waters. Rondeau, Long Point, and Pelee are paradises for us birders who make our pilgrimage to the lake each May, hoping to spot a rare little gull along the beach or a tufted titmouse in the Carolinian forest.

As for Ontario, I live not far from its shores and still remember with gratitude when in sultry summers we escaped the heat by taking the ferry to Toronto Island or the excursion steamer to the mouth of the Niagara. The island—really islands—is still there, much improved, but the cruise ships, alas, are long gone.

The five lakes are the steps in a gigantic staircase whose top step is Superior, a body of water so vast that its volume is greater than all the other lakes put together, with enough water still left over to fill three additional Eries.

Superior tumbles into Huron—the second step in the stairs—by a twenty-one-foot drop, most of it concentrated on a single wild, one-mile stretch of the St. Mary's River. Georgian Bay is separated from the main lake by the spiny ridge of the Bruce Peninsula, which plunges briefly under water to emerge as Manitoulin Island. Some have called Georgian Bay the sixth great lake, but hydrologically it, Lake Michigan, and Huron are a single body of water. There is no drop to separate them; no canal, no locks are needed. The Straits of Mackinac, which connect Michigan and Huron, are just that—straits, not a river.

A mere eight feet below Michigan-Huron lies shallow little Erie, connected to the upper lakes by the St. Clair and Detroit rivers and Lake St. Clair. The drop is so gentle that no man-made ditch or lock is needed here. But Lake Ontario, at the base of the Niagara Escarpment, is three hundred and sixty feet below Erie, cut off from its sister by the cataract of Niagara. In early times such an impediment meant hours of back-breaking portages. It is easy to see why the early traders preferred to skirt this obstacle and go up the Ottawa and down to Georgian Bay by way of Lake Nipissing and the French River. Now a series of locks at the Soo, across the Niagara Peninsula, and along the St.

The five lakes are the steps in a gigantic staircase whose top step is Superior, a body of water so vast that its volume is greater than all the other lakes put together, with enough water still left over to fill three additional Eries.

Just three centuries ago, the Great Lakes supported a little more than one hundred thousand aborigines. Today, some thirty-five million souls from more than one hundred different ethnic groups are crammed into the skyscraper cities (such as Chicago, opposite) that have totally changed the complexion of the five inland seas.

Lawrence has connected all five lakes, making it easy for oceangoing vessels to travel all the way from Liverpool to Duluth. As a later chapter will show, the blessing is not unmixed.

When the first Europeans arrived, a little more than one hundred thousand aboriginal people occupied the eleven thousand miles of what some have called "the fifth coast." Now close to thirty-five million people live along these shores. That represents an extraordinary explosion of population over a period of only four hundred years. It has, of course, meant fundamental changes, not just in the land bordering the lakes but also in the entire continent, for the presence of the lakes is responsible for this huge concentration of people in the continent's heart. Without them the population balance would be quite different. This hypothesis can be a source of endless speculation. What if the Great Lakes had not been carved out by the ice masses of the Pleistocene Age? What if the melt water from the glacier had run off directly into the oceans? In short, what would North America be like if the Great Lakes had never come to be?

One possibility is that under those conditions there would be only one country. The lakes divide the eastern half of the continent into two realms, defying the rest of the natural geography. The mountain ranges and the plains run north and south, but the lakes and the rivers tend to run east and west. These were the continent's first trade routes, well established by tireless men in birch-bark canoes, long before the United States and Canada existed. Thus the lakes acted as a barrier between two peoples: first between the French, who used them to penetrate the heart of the continent, and the British, who stayed closer to the Atlantic shore and to Hudson Bay; later between the Americans and the Canadians, for whom the lakes became a battleground. The 49th parallel is the logical extension of the St. Lawrence–Great Lakes corridor. It helps define the political shape of the continent.

We are separate countries today—separate and distinct—because of a geological phenomenon that once changed the nature of our northern world. In various subtle ways we cannot always comprehend, we are what we are because of the overpowering presence of the largest single source of sweet water on the globe.

CHAPTER ONE

THE MYTHIC ROAD TO TARTARY

This map of New France by the cartographer Coronelli was published in 1688. It was the first to show the Great Lakes in their entirety and was the most accurate general portrayal of the lakes and tributaries in the 17th century.

THE SCHOOLBOOKS I READ AS A BOY PRESENTED THE EARLY EXPLORERS AS BOLD and farseeing adventurers, the "Makers of Canada" ahead of their time. It comes as a bit of a shock to realize that they didn't give two hoots about building a country. It was the wealth of fabled Cathay that lured them on. To them Canada was merely an obstacle full of gloomy, demon-infested forests and wild water that stood in the way of their obsession with the mysterious East. The great inland seas, when they first encountered them, proved to be a disappointment. As Champlain realized, standing on the shore of Georgian Bay, this was not the fabled great South Sea.

Still, they refused to abandon the quest, even when common sense should have told them it was futile—that they were chasing a will-o'-the-wisp. For more than a century they managed to persuade themselves that the great river of the St. Lawrence and the lakes beyond were a pathway leading to the Orient, with its spices, silks, and precious gems.

What made them cling so obsessively to this fantasy? Anyone raised in a placer mining camp, as I was, will understand the eternal, goofy optimism that drives the treasure hunters. I lived among such people. To them the slightest hint of a gold find, no matter how flimsy, was enough to start a mad stampede to nowhere. My own parents bought stock in the Lone Star Mine, which was supposed to unearth the "mother lode" from which all the treasure in the Klondike was said to have its origin. This was as chimerical as the fabled Kingdom of the Saguenay, the Iroquois invention designed to keep Jacques Cartier from invading their hunting grounds. My parents' stock was worthless, of course; the mother lode was never found and is almost certainly nonexistent. Yet men still seek it to this day. Like the explorers of old, they are unflagging in their ardour.

So it was that in July 1634, one full century after Jacques Cartier's arrival at the mouth of the St. Lawrence, we find the myth of a passage to the Orient still very much alive. To be fair to the explorers, none had any idea of the vastness of the new continent or of the real distances involved. To them, it was conceivable that Cathay lay just around the corner.

That July, Jean Nicollet, the thirty-six-year-old "discoverer" of Lake

PARTIE OCCIDENTALE
du CANADA ou de la NOUVELLE
FRANCE
ou sont les Nations des ILINOIS, de TRACY, les
IROQUOIS, et plusieurs autres Peuples;
Auec la LOUISIANE Nouvellement decouverte etc.
Dressée sur les Memoires les plus Nouueaux
Par le P. Coronelli Cosmographe de la Ser.me Repub. de VENISE
Corrigée, et augmentée Par le S.r Tillemon; et Dediée
A Monsieur l'Abbé BAUDRAND.
A PARIS
Chez J.B. Nolin Sur le Quay de l'Horloge du Palais Vers le
Pont Neuf a l'Enseigne de la Place des Victoires.
Auec Priuilege du Roy.
1688.

Michigan, turned up on the shores of Green Bay wearing a magnificent robe of silk damask embroidered with flowers and birds. Convinced that this comic-opera costume was the suitable garment in which to greet the Great Khan of Tartary, the young explorer stepped ashore, his arrival accompanied by a pistol salute from his Huron paddlers. The spectacle caused the local people to prostrate themselves, in the belief that this strange apparition was a god. No doubt to Nicollet's chagrin, they did not look to him like Orientals. They were, rather, Winnebago Indians who lived along those shores.

Yet Nicollet still harboured the lingering hope that China was just over the next hill. He repacked his silken garment and stubbornly followed the Fox River south to the village of the Mascoutens. Alas, the Great Khan was not to be found there either. If the explorer expected him to pop out of the shrubbery with a Fu Manchu moustache and a handful of rubies, he was disappointed. Further travel southward was equally disappointing. Back he went, all the way to Quebec, to inform Samuel de Champlain that he hadn't located a northwest passage. Yet more than two centuries later, such is the power of myth, men were still seeking it in the frozen Arctic. By then other routes to Cathay had long since been found and its treasure unlocked.

This is not the only farcical episode in the history of Great Lakes exploration. Nature, in effect, played a huge joke on the early explorers. Here they were, searching for a fabled land of untold wealth when there was treasure for the taking along the lakes—as easily available and as obvious as a bracelet on an aboriginal arm.

For five thousand years the people of the so-called copper culture, which preceded the woodland culture of Champlain's day, had been mining ingots of pure copper on those shores. Over the years copper trinkets travelled from hand to hand across the continent—all from this source. Cartier was certainly aware that copper was available. At Hochelaga, an Iroquois had pointed to the explorer's silver whistle and his copper-handled dagger and explained that such metals were to be found farther to the west. Cartier paid no heed. Champlain knew about the mineral too, thanks to his protégé, Brûlé, whom he would send west to find the great South Sea. The Algonkians had whetted his curiosity by telling him that Lake Huron, on whose shores he stood, was brackish near the far end.

Brackish! That was enough for Champlain. Off went Brûlé on a quest for salt water. Along the way he came upon some aboriginal copper mines still being worked by natives along Huron's North Channel. But two centuries and more would pass before Lake Superior's pure copper would cause a wild stampede to its shores.

I find Etienne Brûlé the most intriguing figure in the early history of the lakes. He was the first European to see four of them, and it's probable that he also happened by Lake Michigan at the mouth of the Straits of Mackinac. We know little about him. We have no idea what he looked like any more than we know what Champlain or Cartier looked like. The schoolbook portraits are mere artists' inventions.

What a story we would have had if Brûlé had left a series of personal journals! He saw the Great Lakes before Champlain or any other white man. But he could scarcely write his own name, and so, for historians, he remains an enticing if exotic figure, flitting half-seen through the dark forests of the New World.

Brûlé's remarkable feats are obscured by the lack of documentary evidence and by his inconstancy in the war between France and England. If he had any allegiance it was to the Hurons with whom he lived, but even that was misplaced. In his mature years he became bitter and quarrelsome, a change of temperament that contributed to his end. In June 1673, in his home village, a group set upon him, beat him to death, and, so it is said, ate him.

One feels a sense of loss. The first white man to see the lakes could not leave us his story! But Brûlé's encounters with the white world were limited and his reports to Champlain vague and rambling. It has taken the work of many historical detectives to figure out even roughly just where he had gone. He was not a spinner of tales—at least, none has come down to us except one of torture frustrated. He seemed to have accepted his adventures, if he thought of them at all, offhandedly, with no sense of the dramatic. But then it was not his purpose to "discover" anything, merely to roam with his native companions, as free as the winds that gust across the lakes.

Champlain more than made up for Brûlé's failings. He could write and he could draw and it is through his journals, maps, and sketches that we know something of the early history of those waters and the people who lived along their shores.

He has left us with a detailed account of that first journey to Georgian Bay. He and his party took the Ottawa–Nipissing–French River shortcut to Lake Huron, then moved east through the Thirty Thousand Islands until, after four days of paddling, they reached the site of present-day Penetanguishene. Here lay the great domain of the Hurons, a pleasing land of rolling hills, open fields, broad meadows, and stretches of shade trees. Between twenty and thirty

The schoolbooks presented the early explorers as bold, farseeing adventurers. It comes as a bit of a shock to realize that they didn't give two hoots about this country. It was the wealth of fabled Cathay that lured them on.

thousand Indians lived here in palisaded towns and villages. The chief town of the Bear clan, where Champlain stayed, sustained some two hundred bark-covered lodges, each occupied by many families. It was close to being a promised land, this Georgian Bay country, for it abounded in wild fruits and berries. The Indians cultivated corn, squash, and beans, which they traded to the northern tribes for fur. The lake was alive with "monstrously great" trout, sturgeon, and pike. "It is pleasant to travel in this country so fair and fertile it is," Champlain wrote. Succeeding generations have agreed. This is summer cottage country today, crowded with pleasure seekers. But the pike, sturgeon, and trout have long since vanished.

In this favoured realm bordering the *mer douce*, the charitable Hurons helped him build a lodge. A cheerful people, they still had no compunction about torturing their enemies to death; but then, torture was not strange to the explorers from Europe, which had a tradition of burning its own witches and heretics alive.

In Champlain's view, the Hurons were unfortunate in their lack of domestic animals. "Nevertheless with all their wretchedness I consider them a happy people." But he also pitied them because they were heathen. "I reflected that it is a great misfortune that so many creatures should live and die without any knowledge of God and even without any religion or law, whether divine, political, or civil, established among them."

The Father of New France was the complete opposite of Brûlé, who didn't subscribe to any religion or law. Huron society was sexually permissive, a code that Brûlé made the most of wherever he travelled. From puberty onward, young girls took lovers, a practice that scandalized Champlain and the missionaries who followed him. One night in a Huron village near Penetanguishene, he ventured outside his lodge to escape the hordes of fleas within, whereupon "a shameless girl came boldly up to me, offering to keep me company, which I declined with thanks, sending her away with gentle remonstrances...."

Champlain had thrown in his lot—the French lot—with the Hurons in their various wars with the more militant Iroquois, who then lived along the southern shore of Lake Ontario. As most schoolchildren know, the Iroquois, aided by their English allies, eventually won out, and the Huron nation was decimated. But by then Champlain was gone. One of his last acts was to send Jean Nicollet on the mission to seek the way to Tartary. When Nicollet returned to Quebec with his Chinese robe in the fall of 1635, Champlain was on his death bed. He died on Christmas Day.

Yet the dream of a passage to China never quite died. It burned brightly in the mind of a restless young Jesuit, René-Robert Cavelier, who had grown so bored with the Society that he had himself released from his vows, and at the age of twenty-four set off for Canada. The Sieur de La Salle, to give him the name that history accords him, longed to bask in the glory of discovery. He obtained from the Sulpicians a seigneury on the St. Lawrence. There, not far from the rapids that barred the way west, he built a fortified post that he named, flamboyantly, *À La Chine*—"On To China!"—the site of present-day Lachine, Quebec.

On to China he proposed to go. He had heard from the Senecas of a river called the O-hy-o and determined to seek it out "in order not to leave to

***First Sailing of the* Griffin *on Lake Erie, August 7, 1679*, by George Catlin. Paul Mellon Collection, Board of Trustees, National Gallery of Art, Washington, D.C.**

To the Sieur de La Salle, the Great Lakes were the key. In his imagination he could envisage fleets of galleons plying those inland seas, carrying furs from the hinterland and securely establishing the French presence in the heart of the continent.

another the honour of finding the way to the Southern Sea and thereby the route to China." Whether or not he found it is a matter for some speculation. But he did reach Lake Ontario to take over a fort on the site of present-day Kingston. He renamed it Fort Frontenac after the recently appointed governor of New France.

This cost money, and for the rest of his life La Salle was rarely free of debt. But that never stood in the way of his ambitions. The record suggests that he made more enemies than friends. On his various adventures his followers tended to desert him or to mutiny and threaten his life. One nautical historian has dubbed him "the most hated man in North America."

I do not care much for La Salle. He was a man of unbending will, driven by some inner demon that often made him act impetuously. I would not care to have worked for him or followed his lead on his various enterprises, many of which ended in frustration or tragedy. Yet I find it difficult not to admire La Salle's single-mindedness, especially in adversity. Although he, too, wanted to find a route to the fabled Orient, he also had more practical plans. His dream was to seize control of the Great Lakes for France and build a series of forts to oversee a French empire in the heart of the continent. To him the lakes were the key. In his imagination the Sieur de La Salle could envisage fleets of galleons plying those inland seas, carrying furs from the hinterland and securely establishing the French presence in the heart of the continent.

To launch his imperial design he would need a ship. He had already managed to launch two small sailing craft on Lake Ontario, but his ambitions required something sturdier. He would need to launch a barque on the shores of Lake Erie above the implacable barrier of Niagara Falls.

He wasted no time, but disaster dogged him. He was the first to envisage the Great Lakes as a highway on which to carry the natural resources of the hinterland to the settled eastern seaboard and Europe. He put the first vessels on the lakes, but the lakes were his enemy. Even as his men hammered his new barque *Griffon* together, an earlier craft was reduced to splinters by Lake Ontario's mountainous waves. In spite of that setback he managed to finish *Griffon* and sail her all the way across Erie and Huron to Michilimackinac Island (later called Mackinac). There he discovered that his advance party had plundered all his trade goods and fled. He sailed on to Green Bay, loaded his spanking new ship with a fortune in beaver pelts, and sent her off to Niagara only to learn, months later, that she had vanished with all on board.

La Salle's trials pass all comprehension. A man possessed, he searched vainly for his missing ship, all the way down the long corridor of Lake Michigan. He built two forts—part of his grand scheme for a chain of French bastions from the lakes to the Gulf of Mexico. He stumbled back to Lake Erie through a jungle so dense that his men's clothes were torn to shreds and their faces scratched so as to be unrecognizable. But there was no sign of his missing craft. Worse, his supply base on the Niagara had been burned down while a ship from France had been lost at sea with all his trade goods.

He still wouldn't quit. His dream of a fortress chain was shattered when he found that one post had been burned and plundered by the men he left behind while another, on Lake Michigan, had been ravaged. It was clear that his missing ship would never be found and it never has been—the victim, certainly, of a storm like those that would destroy so many other vessels in the years that followed.

In spite of these setbacks, he went on to reach the delta of the Mississippi and to found the new French province of Louisiana. No other man had crammed so much adventure, so much excitement, so many triumphs, and so many heartbreaks into a single career. Though he died at the hands of some of his quarrelling followers in the mud and reeds of the Gulf of Mexico lowlands, he was essentially a man of the lakes, of Ontario and Erie, Huron and Michigan, whose tempestuous waters he had dared time and again in the course of his frustrating and frustrated career.

THE CLAW MARKS OF
THE ICE MONSTER

O N JULY 5, 1848, AT A SMALL BAY ON THE NORTH SHORE OF LAKE SUPERIOR, THERE WAS enacted a curious little scene that seems incongruous yet is so apt. A group of sophisticated white men—nine Harvard scholars, two European naturalists, two New York doctors, and two proper Bostonians—are gazing at the deep scratches in a two-hundred-metre stretch of polished granite, sloping down to the water's edge.

They have come here to this empty inlet by birch-bark canoe and mackinaw boat at the behest of a stocky, voluble Swiss who, much to the bafflement of the native guides, holds their rapt attention. He has seduced them, through the force of his personality, to come here to the back of beyond to look at rocks and fishes and to benefit from the nightly chalk talks he gives with the aid of a portable blackboard.

It is a long way to come for a lecture, but this is no ordinary professor. He is one of the world's most celebrated scientists, the great Louis Agassiz, whose "*Eiszeit*" theory, scarcely a decade old, has plunged him into a whirlwind of controversy and cost him personal friendships. Agassiz keeps insisting that the northern hemisphere, almost from the Pole to the Mediterranean, was once completely covered by an enormous glacier.

Now, here he is at one of the many stops on his Lake Superior odyssey, explaining that this piece of sloping granite, which seems to have been smoothed by a gigantic polisher and subjected to the claw marks of some monstrous beast, proves once again his Ice Age theory. He has seen the same kind of striated rocks before in his native Switzerland, and they confirm his belief that most of North America, too, was once smothered by a mantle of ice. Here, on this bay, are the clear tracks of the receding ice sheet.

When Agassiz's theory was made public, more than three centuries after Jacques Cartier reached North America, it profoundly disturbed those who still believed in the Biblical deluge. One distinguished scientist, Sir George Mackenzie, actually read a paper before the Royal Society in which he maintained that all the appearances that Agassiz referred to as the work of glaciers—the vast gravel ridges, the kettle-like depressions in sand plains, the polished and striated rock—were caused by blocks of ice that floated and drifted about as the result of the Biblical flood. (Oddly, the word "drift" is still used by geologists to describe the wide variety of deposits left by the ice sheets.)

Yet Agassiz himself clung to the catastrophic theory of creation—that species develop through repeated cataclysmic occurrences. In effect, he replaced the idea of a worldwide flood with that of a worldwide glacier. He was no

Darwinian evolutionist: the catastrophe of the Ice Age, he was convinced, was divinely inspired. When *Origin of Species* was published, Agassiz rejected it.

Even those who disagreed were charmed by him. When he arrived to take a Harvard professorship not long before his Lake Superior trip he was lionized. He enjoyed the friendship and admiration of the leading men of letters and science, from Ralph Waldo Emerson to Henry Wadsworth Longfellow, a dinner companion who found him "a pleasant voluble man, with a bright gleaming face." His reputation was such that the great editor Horace Greeley refused to publish an attack on him by an amateur naturalist, warning the writer of the futility of tangling with such a distinguished scientist.

Although Agassiz's *Eiszeit* theory was shown by later research to be simplistic, it was to change drastically our view of the past. It helped explain the odd occurrence of house-sized boulders, the vast deposits of sand and gravel, and the snakelike ridges that we can see today in the hinterland of the Great Lakes.

The striations that Agassiz showed his disciples on Superior's granite

shore ran north and west, pointing to that spot in the Keewatin Region where the last of the great ice sheets—the Laurentide—had its birth, some sixty thousand years earlier, during the Wisconsin glaciation. An ice sheet does not advance in one direction. It oozes outward from its centre, like molasses poured from a jug. It may begin as a small patch of one winter's snow, which, by the time the sun's rays weaken in the fall, has not entirely melted. As the patch continues to build, the pressure of its own weight metamorphoses it into ice. More snow falls; more ice forms. The glacier begins to expand, imperceptibly, until it becomes a great white monster, creeping across the land, smothering everything—forests, plains, lakes, rivers—in a mantle of ice as much as two miles thick.

Agassiz thought in terms of a single ice age—a period when a massive frozen wall crept down from the polar regions and then, after many millennia, crept back. We now know that the story of the ice ages is immensely more complicated. Agassiz's belief in one catastrophic worldwide glacier has long since been shot down. Geologists have figured out that within these long chilly epochs the temperature rose and fell many times, creating mini-ice ages interspersed with long periods of warmth.

It is this smaller ebb and flow within a larger ebb and flow that is so confusing. When I first began to study the onslaught of the ice in northern Canada, conventional theory held that there were four ice ages. Modern scientific theory, finds this, too, simplistic.

The statistics of the great glacial advances and retreats are hard to comprehend. We now know that in the past two and a half million years—the Pleistocene period—there have been dozens of "glaciations," each one lasting upward of fifty thousand years, interspersed with shorter interglacial periods when the climate grew warmer. One of these interglacial periods is our own. It reached its peak some ten thousand years ago when the Great Lakes were formed. It is now about half over. Some five thousand years from now, if man has not manipulated geological history, the ice will once again begin to creep down from the polar regions and the northern half of the continent will be changed out of all recognition.

The Great Lakes are the product of the Laurentide ice sheet, the last of many "glaciations" that successively covered the northern half of the continent beginning in the Pleistocene period. When the Laurentide sheet began its inexorable advance, the Great Lakes did not exist. The region, however, was in general a basin for the shallow seas that covered the land, leaving behind a number of the world's greatest salt deposits, some of them half a mile thick—enough, it is said, to supply all the world forever—concealed under a blanket of limestone.

This so-called Michigan Basin lay on the southern edge of the Precambrian Shield and was itself composed of a series of depressions, all stacked like saucers, one on top of the other. The saucer-shaped layers, being made up of limestone from sediments laid down in the seas, were softer than the granites of the Shield to the north. When the seas drained away and the ice came down, each successive sheet—the Nebraskan, followed by the Kansan, followed by the Illinoian, followed by the Wisconsin—sliced off a layer, exposing another one hidden below.

Before our present era, rivers undoubtedly flowed through this depression, valleys were formed, and, for all we know, other lakes existed. But each ice sheet destroyed that evidence and eroded the bedrock still deeper. Scientists have nonetheless been able to chart the flows and ebbs of the most recent ice sheet and its relation to the Great Lakes by studying the contents of glacial moraines, searching out old beach patterns, examining the strata in the rock formations, and establishing time periods through carbon dating.

The Laurentide ice sheet nosed its way south in fits and starts, retreating or advancing as the climate changed, until the entire Great Lakes region as we know it today vanished under a mountain of ice. The glacier reached its most southerly point some distance below the 40th parallel along the present Ohio River, eighteen thousand years ago. By that time it had covered all of our Lake Michigan, including the present site of Chicago. Then, as the weather warmed again, it began to melt at the edges.

As the ice retreated, it left exposed the evidence of its arrival and departure, including the grooves in the granite that Agassiz had shown his students. These were created by rocks borne along under the moving glacier that acted like tools to score the surface of the rock. There were also vast ridges of sand and stones, known as moraines, bulldozed south by the advancing ice, and a group of oddly shaped mounds and embankments with elfin names, such as *eskers* (long, sinuous spines that marked the passing of subglacial streams); *drumlins* (streamlined hills in parallel, pointing in the direction of the glacier's flow); *kames* (hillocks of glacial debris); and *kettles* (little round lakes created by melting blocks of ice that had tumbled off the three-thousand-foot face of the glacial wall). Over the years many of these manifestations have been mined for their sand and gravel. Some can be seen today, such as the famous Oak

The glacier begins to expand, imperceptibly, until it becomes a great white monster, creeping across the land, smothering everything—forests, plains, lakes, rivers—in a mantle of ice as much as two miles thick.

35

Ridges moraine north of Toronto. I have driven many times along the esker that parallels the north shore of Lake Erie east of Point Pelee and does duty as a highway embankment.

The history of this period, which began about 13,500 years ago, is, to say the least, confusing. The meltwater that poured off the glacial cliffs collected in the great hollows along the margin of the Shield, and—in the case of Lake Superior—on the hard rock of the Shield itself. Lakes began to form on the rim of the ice sheet as soon as it began its long retreat.

As it crawled back, the great glacier acted as a dike to retain the runoff water and create new lakes while opening spillways to drain others into the ocean. Some lakes expanded into vast seas, bigger than the present ones; others contracted into rivers, coalesced with other lakes, or vanished entirely. For twelve millennia or more the entire territory was in a state of flux. The land itself, previously compressed by the weight of the ice, began to rise like a sponge as the melting process continued.

I think of the ice as a living entity—a restless creature that surges forward, hesitates, retreats, hesitates again, and then repeats its slow cycle, its fingers sometimes stretching out for hundreds of miles to claw at the ravaged land. But this is to suggest perceptible movement, while to those aboriginals who hunted on the glacier's rim, these frozen cliffs must have seemed eternally immobile. It was scarcely possible, even over a lifetime, to detect any change, any suggestion of advance or retreat. And what a spectacle it must have been!

The monstrous wall of glittering blue ice was slowly melting, its forward edge, soiled with the grime of ages, now sloping downward to the moraines it had created. These vast, fan-shaped deserts of silt and rubble were pocked with ponds and veined with instant rivers, winding, serpent-fashion, toward a distant sea.

The ice did not retreat on an even front. Great frozen tongues, known as lobes, jutted out from the main glacial sheet. One huge lobe filled the entire depression that would eventually hold Lake Michigan. At its foot, little Lake Chicago had already taken shape.

Farther to the east, the ancestor of Lake Erie was born in the shadow of the ice cliffs. A thousand years later both of these meltwater ponds had grown and changed shape. Lake Erie's ancestor had expanded to twice the size of the modern lake. Lake Chicago by then covered the lower half of what is now Lake Michigan. At the same time Lake Huron's ancestor was slowly emerging.

Another ten thousand years passed, and once again the lake country was transformed. Lake Superior still slumbered under its crushing mantle of ice. Lake Chicago, now an immense sheet of meltwater, covered most of the present sites of Huron and Michigan. But Lake Erie's ancestor was reduced to two small ponds because the land, no longer depressed by the ice, was rising again.

If we fast-forward geological time, as on a video recorder, we can see this drama of lakes expanding and shrinking and draining away. The ice dammed up the St. Lawrence River, forcing the ancestor of Lake Ontario to drain down the Hudson River depression. But now another spectacular lake began to form, so enormous that it makes the present-day lakes seem shrunken. This vast body of freshwater, by far the largest in history, spread over most of modern Manitoba, Minnesota, and North Dakota as well as large parts of Ontario and Quebec. It has been named, quite properly, for Louis Agassiz. When at last it shrank to its present site and size it became Lake Winnipeg.

Meanwhile Lake Superior began to emerge from its long gestation. Two small ponds appeared on the glacier's southern rim. As the centuries moved on, they grew until Superior began to assume the shape we know today. At the same time Erie and Ontario took on now-familiar contours. The meltwater that had filled the entire Michigan Basin began to drain into the shallow sea that filled the valley of the St. Lawrence. The ancestor of Michigan-Huron also shrank as the ice sheet moved north, for there was no longer enough melt-water to support its size.

As the surviving lakes took their present shape, they were fed, not by the melting glacier, but by the streams and rivers that emerged in the new drainage basin left behind by the ice sheet. Once the St. Lawrence was freed of ice, all five lakes drained into it. But to the north, Lake Agassiz was doomed. As the ice abandoned it, this vast sheet of water shrank and was gobbled up by Hudson Bay. No other glacial lake approached it in size: a Great Lake indeed, albeit short-lived, an appropriate memorial to the barrel-chested Swiss scientist who first glimpsed the wonders of the Ice Age in the riven granite of two continents.

The Niagara Escarpment, seen here on the Bruce Peninsula, goes back far beyond the ice age. It was created by the remains of small creatures accumulating over the eons when a shallow ocean covered the region.

Shorelines

Wind, water, and moving
ice have sculptured the
shores of the five inland
seas, creating on nature's
canvas, vistas that range
from the tempestuous
to the sublime.

*Two contrasting views taken at
Michigan's Pictured Rocks National
Lakeshore, which hugs the Superior
shoreline for more than forty miles but
is never wider than three miles.*

Lake Huron's Thirty Thousand Islands adorn Georgian Bay. The extent of natural erosion can be seen close up at Flowerpot Island, part of Fathom Five National Marine Park.

ABOVE: One of the Thirty Thousand Islands as seen from the air. The shack is deserted.
RIGHT: The setting sun colours the usually gloomy Agawa Rocks,
Agawa Bay, Lake Superior.

OVERLEAF: The Scarborough Bluffs have for years been a Mecca for
picnicking Torontonians.

TOP: *Part of the world-famous Indiana Dunes on Lake Michigan, an hour's drive from Chicago, were rescued after a fifty-year-long conservation battle.*
ABOVE: *The shore of Point Pelee National Park, Ontario, seen at dawn when both birds and birders are up and moving.*

RIGHT: *Michigan's Sleeping Bear Dunes provide an ever-unfolding vista that may change more than once within a human life span.*

CHAPTER THREE

THE FEATS OF THE PORK-EATERS

W HEN I WAS A YOUNG INFANTRY RECRUIT DURING THE SECOND WORLD WAR, I was introduced to a particular form of torture known as the route march. It was one of several devices the army used to whip us city boys into shape. We marched, generally on concrete highways, for five miles, each carrying a thirty-pound pack. Later on, when some of the softness was gone from our bodies, the miles were lengthened to ten and our packs increased to sixty pounds. How tough we thought we'd become! Fighting fit and fit to fight: "hard muscled," to use the newspaper phrase. But we never liked those exhausting marches. "We'll laugh at all this years from now," my friend Harry Filion used to say wryly as he puffed along beside me. He was right in a way. When I read of the deeds of the voyageurs in the days of the fur trade, I have to laugh at our youthful conviction that this was hard work. History tells me it was really child's play.

In the pantheon of remarkable human specimens created during the long evolutionary march from caveman to capitalist, the French-Canadian voyageur stands near the pinnacle. I find it exhausting just to read about him. Is there any human being on earth today who could match him for strength or endurance? The voyageurs were, in every sense of the word, supermen. Until they appeared on Canadian waters there was nothing remotely like them. Nor has there been anything like them since. The American fur king, John Jacob Astor, was speaking nothing less than the truth when he said that a single Canadian voyageur was worth three ordinary paddlers.

Frederick Graham, a young Englishman who travelled with the Hudson's Bay governor George Simpson, described them in 1847—short, thick, tireless men who resembled "fiends" in the oppressive heat, "their shirts off, their skins like heated copper and their long black hair all loose, with their wild, black eyes glowing like hot coals."

Few were more than five feet six inches tall because nobody larger could fit easily into a canoe. They had tremendous shoulders and arms, for on the roughest portages they never carried less than one hundred and eighty pounds. Some carried twice that much, and at least one man is credited with

ABOVE: **Looking down on Lake Superior at the reconstructed fort at Grand Portage, Minnesota.**
RIGHT: **Frances Ann Hopkins, a nineteenth-century artist, produced the best-known paintings of the voyageur period, shown here and on the following pages. This is** *Shooting the Rapids.*

The upper lakes resounded to the slap of hundreds of paddles as the members of that unique Canadian breed, the voyageurs, propelled themselves along the shorelines of Superior and Huron in big bark canoes loaded with pelts.

humping *five* ninety-pound packages of trade goods on his back—well over twice his weight—as he trotted through the forest tangle.

Ninety-pound packs! And each man carried a minimum of two. It makes my memory of those sixty-pound route marches look silly. Did they stagger under the weight of their crushing burdens? Did they gasp as Harry and I did? Far from it. They didn't walk; *they ran!* Time was of the essence in the short summer season. Every moment counted if the furs were to be transshipped at the western rendezvous and brought by canoe to Montreal in time for shipment to Europe. Onto their shoulders they hoisted these incredible loads, secured by a tumpline around their foreheads, and dogtrotted the full distance. Ordinary men who carried little or nothing found it hard to keep up with them. They brought everything to Grand Portage on Superior's western shore—everything, from canoes, kegs of liquor, and portable stoves to bales of blankets and sacks of trinkets for their Indian suppliers. At Grand Portage they exchanged these for bales of furs, Canada's first great natural resource, and headed back toward Montreal. The vision of Cathay and its treasure had dimmed by the time the eighteenth century dawned. In the forests beyond the lakes there was greater wealth and, thanks to a unique Canadian invention, the French had the means of getting there. The canoe helped to give Canada its horizontal structure.

The first Canadian fortunes were not founded on hordes of gold or precious stones. They were carved out of three elements of the natural environment—beaver, birch bark, and freshwater. It was this happy juxtaposition that created the first Canadian industry. La Salle's vision came true when the upper lakes resounded to the slap of hundreds of paddles as the voyageurs propelled themselves along the shorelines of Superior and Huron in big bark canoes loaded with pelts.

The beaver is properly our national symbol. When the first Europeans arrived there were at least ten million of these industrious rodents in North America. The French reached the lakes at a propitious moment. Canada would thrive on a quirk of the European fashion trade. An undercoat of soft wool beneath the beavers' glossy pelts produced a felt that, stiffened with shellac, could be moulded into any shape, from topper to tricorne. Every well-to-do European wanted a beaver hat. Small wonder that by the mid-seventeenth century the animals were virtually gone from the St. Lawrence. And so the fur trade moved west into the vast forested realm beyond the lakes.

Those shadowy figures the coureurs de bois, who lived like Indians and trapped the beaver illicitly, were in the vanguard. They were, in effect, tax evaders who ventured into the wilderness without the licences required by the colonial government. They thumbed their noses at authority and surreptitiously supplied Quebec merchants with pelts. When young Pierre Radisson and his brother-in-law, Médard Chouart Des Groseilliers, arrived in Montreal with a fortune in furs from the head of the lakes, they were slapped with a fine so monstrous they took their expertise to the English and helped found the Hudson's Bay Company.

With the end of the French regime in 1763, the independent coureur de bois gradually disappears from history. He was followed in the same tradition by that other genuine Canadian creation, the voyageur, who was, however, a hired hand working for one of the big fur companies. Voyageurs needed seven thousand calories a day to maintain their killing pace—more than twice the amount required by a modern adult male. I do not envy them their diet, but it seemed to do the trick. Their staple food consisted of a mush made of dried beans, salt pork, and sea biscuit. They rose at three each morning and made the first leg of the day's journey on empty stomachs. They breakfasted after dawn, then paddled until nine or ten at night, driving their big canoes at the rate of between forty and sixty paddle strokes a minute. The mind is boggled. One might expect them to pant their way along the lakes and down the rivers. In fact, they *sang*. Lustily. Some of these songs have come down to us today— "En roulant ma boule"…"Alouette." The rhythm, matching each paddle stroke, seemed to drive them on.

Thomas L. McKenney, who made the trip in a voyageur canoe across Lake Superior, recorded that he asked his men at seven one night if it wasn't time for them to beach their canoe and go ashore for the evening. "They answered they were fresh yet. They had been constantly paddling since three o'clock this morning—57,600 strokes with the paddles—and 'fresh yet.' No human beings, except the Canadian French, could stand this. Encamped…at half-past nine o'clock, having come today *seventy-nine miles.*"

The history of early Canada is inextricably entwined with the birch-bark canoe, a product of the gloomy boreal forest that covered most of the country. It has been observed that Canada is one of those rare lands in which the horse was not the original provider of transportation. No four-footed beast of burden could operate in the land of the great lakes, broken rock, heaving

OVERLEAF: In her *Canoes in the Fog, Lake Superior, 1869*, Hopkins captured the mystique of voyageur travel. In this painting and also in that on pages 56-57, she included herself as a passenger in the great canoe.

muskeg, and primeval forest. The day had not yet arrived when successors to La Salle's *Griffon* would navigate the inland seas; for most of a century the canoe reigned supreme.

No other craft was flexible enough to run the rapids or light enough to be carried on men's backs. And the building materials lay close at hand. A single paper birch could supply enough bark for one canoe. Thin strips of white cedar formed the ribs. The boiled gum of the spruce was the glue that held it all together. There wasn't a nail or any other piece of metal in the entire craft.

The largest of these—*canot de maître*, known as the Montreal canoe—weighed six hundred pounds wet, was thirty-six feet long, five feet wide at the centre, and carried a crew of ten. In these swift craft the "pork-eaters" from the East rendezvoused with the winterers from the Northwest, who travelled in the smaller, lighter *canot du nord*. But before the *mangeurs de lard* arrived at the foot of the Grand Portage to exchange trade goods for furs, they stopped at Pointe aux Chapeaux to wash and preen themselves, for they were all great dandies. Their distinctive dress consisted of moose-skin moccasins (without socks), corduroy trousers secured at the knee with beaded garters and held up by the famous crimson sash, and a sky-blue hooded coat or *capot* with brass buttons.

They were joined by a fierce common bond. They knew they belonged to a unique breed, and they revelled in it. Pride in physical prowess drove them to incredible feats. There were instances in which voyageurs paddled for forty-eight hours without stopping in order to beat out another canoe in a race for which there was no prize. They hated to admit defeat. Canoe racing upstream was one of their chief delights. A young Chicago scientist, Robert Kennicott, wrote how the act of moving against the current rather than with it put his paddlers in high good humour: "...the canoes were constantly contending for the lead, the relative cleverness of the bowsmen in cutting off the bends in the river . . . causing much excitement and sport."

It seems a life of drudgery to us, but for the men who endured it and flourished in it, it was the only life. Here is an old voyageur looking back on his life with satisfaction and pride: "For twenty-four years I was a light canoeman. . . . No portage was too long for me; all portages were alike. My end of the canoe never touched the ground till I saw the end [of the portage]. . . . Fifty songs a day were nothing to me, I could carry, paddle, walk and sing with any man I ever saw. . . . No water, no weather, ever stopped the paddle or the

Canoes in a Fog, Lake Superior, 1869, Frances Ann Hopkins, Glenbow Collection, Calgary, Canada

song. . . . I wanted for nothing; and I spent all my earnings in the enjoyment of pleasure. Five hundred pounds, twice told, have passed through my hands; although now I have not a spare shirt to my back, nor a penny to buy one. Yet, were I young again, I should glory in commencing the same career again. I would spend another half-century in the same fields of enjoyment. . . . There is no life so happy as a voyageur's life; none so independent; no place where a man enjoys so much variety and freedom as in the Indian country."

You can follow the track of the voyageurs by studying the place-names along Superior's armoured shores: Pancake Bay, Bottle Point, and, more irreverently, Les Mamelles and Cape Gargantua. The canoes travelled in brigades, as many as thirty together, following the beautiful North Channel of Lake Huron. Those heading south down Lake Michigan stopped at Michili-mackinac, an important depot for repositioning cargo. Those heading for Grand Portage, or later Fort William, stopped at Sault Ste Marie, and here, resplendent in sashes and plumes, held high carnival day and night with the compliant young Indian women. Many who had lost as much as fifteen pounds on the long portage route to the lake now put it back on even more rapidly, causing one traveller to remark, after a three-day stop, that some "became so much improved in looks that it was difficult to recognize our voyageurs."

Along Superior's four hundred miles of shoreline the canoes were never far from land, for the lake is subject to sudden squalls that could swamp any craft and fogs that can screen the land. The north shore is riven by deep bays, and many voyageurs were tempted to take advantage of the shortcut from headland to headland, a practice fraught with peril, for the waves on the open lake are the size of ocean breakers. Often, to escape the wind, they paddled by night. Sometimes when a bad squall came up suddenly, they streaked for one of the innumerable bays that served as safe harbours. Sometimes when *La Vieille*—the old lady, as they called the wind—blew in the right direction they hoisted square sails and skimmed at eight or ten knots along the coast. In adverse winds they took to the shore, laid out their packs to dry, and relaxed. But they paid for these idle moments. In the great days of the fur trade a canoe was pinned down in the summer an average of one day in three—time that had to be made up later by intensive paddling.

On the far western shore of Superior, nestled below a great cliff, lay the busiest community in the Northwest. This was Grand Portage, named for the

The voyageurs were joined by a fierce common bond. They knew they belonged to a unique breed, and they revelled in it. Pride in physical prowess drove them to incredible feats.

long and difficult passage that circumvented the falls and rapids of the lower Pigeon River. For the winterers who came from as far away as Athabasca, this portage was a horror. It ran for eight and a half miles—probably the longest carrying place in North America.

Here at the end of the portage was the throbbing heart of the eighteenth-century fur trade, the busiest spot west of the Appalachians, the great cross-roads that linked the lake country with the wild hinterland. Here, on Superior's hostile shore, the Ojibwa Indians, who controlled the trade and acted as middlemen, exacted tribute from those who used the portage trail. By mid-July Grand Portage buzzed with activity as more and more men from the interior arrived and more and more brigades from Montreal poured in. At least a thousand men would be gathered at one time within the palisaded fort that sprang up at the water's edge in the mid-1700s.

The pace here was frantic, for all were working against time. It took a fortnight to move everything over the portage. Then the paddlers had to load

In their *canot de maître*, eight brightly clad voyageurs propel themselves past the rocky ramparts and tumbling cataracts of Superior, with their woman passenger and her companion.

up and head back. The network of rivers and lakes that stretched off as far as the Athabasca country would in a few months be frozen and impassible. Some winterers had to travel two thousand miles to their bases, so that not everyone could return to his post in a single season. The pork-eaters, who faced the long stretch east across two of the Great Lakes and a dozen portages, knew that time was money. At Montreal everything had to be sorted and repacked in order to ship the harvest to England the same year.

In its early days Grand Portage was described as "a pent up hornet's nest of conflicting factions intrenched [*sic*] in rival forts." But by 1779, when the Great Lakes were closed to private shipping as a result of the American Revolution, trade was consolidated. The nine largest merchants formed the nucleus of what was soon to become the North West Company, a loose association that has been likened to a modern cartel. With the revolution over, the new company expanded. By the mid-eighties, it had launched four ships on the lakes, including, in 1793, the big five-ton sloop *Otter*.

The voyageurs rarely camped before nine at night and were up again at three. This strenuous routine required seven thousand calories daily per man.

By this time, too, the North West Company had decided to move its headquarters. The new boundaries established after the American Revolution left Grand Portage on the U.S. side of the border. A new post, Fort William, was built in 1803 at the mouth of the Kaministikwia River, thirty miles north of Grand Portage. A long-forgotten route of the French traders was reopened to join the old Portage route.

Fort William became the summer rendezvous for the fur trade, far grander than its predecessor. All but abandoned in the winter months, it vibrated with life by mid-July as two thousand North West employees, Indians, Scots, Métis, and English poured in.

Washington Irving described the annual assembly at Fort William when two or three of the leading Montreal partners would discuss the company's affairs with partners from the wilderness posts. "Now the aristocratic character of the Briton shone forth magnificently or rather the ducal spirit of the Highlanders." Each wilderness partner had a score of retainers at his beck and call. This gathering was the greatest event of the year, the Montreal partners outdoing themselves in ostentation. "They ascended the rivers in great state . . . like Highland chieftains navigating their subject lakes. They wrapped themselves in rich furs, brought their own cooks and bakers with them, and indulged in delicacies and rich wines rarely seen in the wilderness."

An immense frame building formed the nucleus of the flourishing community on the banks of Lake Superior. Here were the council hall and also the banqueting chamber, built to seat two hundred revellers. Proceedings were conducted in great state: "...every member felt as if sitting in Parliament, and every retainer and dependant looked up to the assemblage with awe, as to the House of Lords." The feasting that accompanied these meetings resembled that in a Highland castle. In the banquet hall the tables, set with English crystal, Irish linen, and Chinese porcelain, groaned under the weight of venison and fish, buffalo tongues and beaver tails. Toast followed toast, pipers played, fiddlers fiddled. The rafters rang with ribaldry and wassail.

"Their merriment was echoed and prolonged by a mongrel legion of retainers, Canadian voyageurs, half-breeds, Indian hunters, and vagabond hangers-on who feasted sumptuously on the crumbs that fell from their tables and made the welkin ring with old French ditties, mingled with Indian yelps...."

The era of the Grand Rendezvous, as it was called, was short-lived. The first gathering was held in 1803, but eighteen years later the Nor'Westers became part of the Hudson's Bay Company—the first great business merger in Canada—and though the fort continued to operate in a minor way, the Grand Rendezvous was finished. William McGillivray, the former chieftain of the Nor' Westers, who had presided over more than one convivial banquet, visited the fort in 1821 and was saddened by what he saw. "The fur trade is forever lost to Canada," he said. Over the next half century the fort fell into disrepair; the dining hall became a shed for canoes; the old blockhouse fell to pieces.

In 1971, the Ontario government made plans to restore this piece of history. A replica of the Great Hall was reopened to visitors a decade later, perfect in every detail except for one small change. The new building does not stand on the original site at the mouth of the Kaministikwia River, where the old one could once be seen in all its glory by the incoming brigades of Montreal canoes. That famous site had been overrun by private houses and a railway yard. The replica had to be moved upstream, where no sensible Nor' Wester would ever have thought of locating it.

All but abandoned in the winter months, Fort William vibrated with life by mid-July as two thousand North West employees, Indians, Scots, Métis, and English poured in.

Strategic Mackinac

In 1812 the fort's guns dominated the upper lakes. It was so far from civilization that its American defenders didn't know war had been declared—until a force of voyageurs and Indians seized it in a surprise attack.

ABOVE: *The island has been a favourite for tourists who come to enjoy the architecture and the flavour of the past.*

LEFT: *This is the view the British forces had as they approached at dawn in July 1812. A mini-Gibraltar, the island guarded the straits between Lakes Huron and Michigan.*

The dominant building on the island is the Grand Hotel, which opened in 1885. Perched on a high bluff overlooking the strait, with its 660-foot verandah, it still displays some of the essence of the grand old days of luxury travel. Horse-drawn carriages (BELOW) maintain the illusion.

LEFT: On the south shore of the strait, facing the island, is Fort Michilimackinac, built by the French in the mid-seventeenth century and a centre of the fur trade for fifty years. The British took it in 1761, lost it to the great chief Pontiac in 1763, reoccupied it a year later, but abandoned it in 1779 and built Fort Mackinac on the island.
BELOW: Children skip stones in the strait, now spanned by the international bridge in the background.

ABOVE: The Cheboygan lighthouse nearby serves to remind us of the power of the storms, one of which probably sent La Salle's Griffon to her doom.

CHAPTER FOUR

THE WAR TO CONTROL THE LAKES

WHO OWNS THE GREAT LAKES?

If that was a question in the early history of Canada, it was not really settled until the outcome of the War of 1812 confirmed that the international border should run down the geographical centre of four of the inland seas. These are international waters today—as, in a sense, they have always been. Although the various aboriginal tribes who occupied the shores did not have the European notions of ownership and "real estate," they did fight territorial wars, such as the long-drawn-out Dakota-Ojibwa conflict up to the mid-eighteenth century. As a result of it, the Ojibwa nation came close to "owning" the waters around Grand Portage. They extracted tolls from the fur traders, who paid them without much protest, thereby conceding the natives' control of the territory. The British, who succeeded the French, found that they, too, had to treat with the various Great Lakes tribes after the Ottawa chief Pontiac and his native followers seized their western outposts and took control of the upper lakes.

The War of 1812 wrote finis to all this. In that fruitless conflict there were no winners, only losers, and the greatest losers were the native peoples. They were scarcely mentioned in the Treaty of Ghent that settled the war, confirmed the boundary through the lakes, and left the shores open to an onrush of white settlers who would, in the years that followed, transform the landscape.

Much of the fighting took place along these waters. Toronto's position on Lake Ontario, back when the town was known as York (sometimes Muddy York), made it vulnerable to the American fleet. Sackets Harbor in New York State acted as a jumping-off point for the abortive attempt on Montreal. The great lake bastions—Fort Niagara, Fort George, and Fort Erie—were central to the conflict. The naval encounter on Lake Erie, the only one ever fought on Canadian waters, was a major turning point. My own view is that the presence of the lakes and the rivers that connect them saved us from becoming a part of the American empire because they acted as a bulwark against successful invasion—Canada's English Channel, in a sense.

Whoever controlled the lakes controlled the war. For Canada, they formed the main line of communication, and that was a distinct advantage. Isaac Brock, the British general, was able to dispatch couriers in fast canoes

ABOVE: **Fort Mackinac restored. Here the first shots in the lake war were fired in July 1812 against the unsuspecting Americans. OPPOSITE: Commodore Oliver Hazard Perry leaves his sinking flagship *Lawrence*, and rows across to *Niagara* to fight on. The painting hangs in the U.S. Capitol building, Washington.**

along the great water highway. It was some of these couriers who brought the news of the war to St. Joseph Island, his outpost at the far end of Lake Huron, while the nearby Americans snored in their bunks. What a way to begin a war! The U.S. garrison at Michilimackinac had no idea, in July 1812, that their country had been at war for a month.

Brock was aware that the island controlled the three upper lakes. Shaped like an aboriginal arrowhead and lying at the juncture of Lakes Michigan and Huron, it was the most strategic piece of real estate on the continent, as Pontiac had understood years before. Brock meant to seize it, and thanks to fast water communication he got it.

For the motley crew of voyageurs and tribesmen who stole across Lake Huron at night to take the island by surprise, it was a bloodless victory. Now the British, in control of this great lump of Precambrian schist, were assured mastery of the fur country. Every craft moving southwest—toward Green Bay or to the Fox-Wisconsin portage or to the upper reaches of the Mississippi— must come within the reach of its guns. Having secured this western anchor, Brock could turn his attention to events closer to home.

Those of us who drive along the parkway from the Falls to Niagara-on-the-Lake have seen the Tuscan pillar atop Queenston Heights that marks the victorious battle in which Brock died. It was said at the time to be the tallest monument in the world, taller even than Nelson's in Trafalgar Square. But those of us who travel in May out to Pelee Island—"Canada's Deep South"— can see in the hazy distance on Erie's southern shore a pillar twice as high as Brock's. It is dedicated to Oliver Hazard Perry, who, in 1813, won for the United States its first decisive victory in this foolish and senseless conflict.

One cannot begrudge the Americans their moment of exultation. After fifteen months of fighting, Perry was the first, indeed the only, hero they had. His triumphant dispatch at the end of the Battle of Lake Erie—"We have met the enemy, and they are ours"—went into the history books. More significantly, his victory forced Britain to abandon its hold on Michigan Territory and to retreat eastward to face a second defeat at the Battle of the Thames.

I have often speculated on the shape Canada would have taken had the British won the Battle of Lake Erie. With those waters lost to the Americans, and with Detroit remaining in British hands, would the international border today run through the centre of the lakes, or would Canada extend farther south, encompassing portions of Pennsylvania, Ohio, and Michigan and perhaps making Canadian cities out of Buffalo, Cleveland, and Detroit?

It is possible, because the Battle of Lake Erie, to paraphrase the Duke of Wellington in another context, was "a near run thing." Either side might have won. Indeed, the British were minutes from victory when the tide suddenly turned. The whole contest smacks of the ridiculous—fifteen wooden sailing ships blasting away at each other in the heart of a wilderness lake, five hundred crow's-flight miles from saltwater. Equally remarkable was the fact that most of these fighting ships were built on these very shores from gigantic trees felled on the spot. Some were scarcely completed before they went into action, for the Battle of Lake Erie was first and foremost a shipbuilding contest.

Perry knew he had to get his vessels built, rigged, and out of Presque Isle Bay, Pennsylvania, before the British could bottle him up. Robert Barclay, the one-armed captain in charge of the British fleet at Amherstburg, could not attack until his own flagship, *Detroit*, and two new gunboats were in the water. Perry also knew that until he completed his two big brigs, *Lawrence* and *Niagara*, he would be outgunned.

One prospect disturbed Perry. The British ships were armed with long guns, the Americans with shorter, more powerful carronades. It was essential, then, that the Americans fight at close quarters. If Perry's fleet was too far from the British, it would be torn to pieces by the long-range cannons.

On the morning of September 10, 1813, the battle began. Perry's lookout, high up on the mast of his flagship, *Lawrence*, spotted the British fleet sneaking past behind a cluster of islands. Almost at that very moment the wind changed in Perry's favour. With the wind behind him he was in a far better position to manoeuvre. Now he could bear down directly on the British fleet. But Barclay's strategy was clear. He would concentrate the entire firepower of his fleet— thirty-four guns—on battering Perry's flagship to pieces before she could get into range. It was not until 12:15 that Perry was close enough to bring up his powerful carronades.

What a spectacle it must have been to those dark, aboriginal eyes, peering through the foliage on shore! The tumult aboard the American flagship was appalling. Perry's thirty-two-pound carronades sprayed the decks of Barclay's flagship while *Lawrence* reeled under the British hammer blows.

Now Barclay suffered a setback. His second most powerful ship, *Queen Charlotte*, lost her captain and two chief officers, with only an inexperienced marine lieutenant left in charge. At those close quarters, it was almost equivalent to sinking.

All around Perry men were dying, but he seemed to bear a charmed life.

One prospect disturbed Perry. The British ships were armed with long guns; the Americans with shorter, more powerful carronades. It was essential that Perry fight at close quarters. If his fleet was too far from the British, it would be torn to pieces.

Not so his flagship. By half past two *Lawrence* was a shambles. She lay like a log in the water, her guns silent.

On the *Detroit*, a wound in the thigh put Barclay out of action. His ship, too, had taken a dreadful pummelling, but the tide seemed to have turned in his favour. The British could see *Lawrence* strike her flag, but Perry had no intention of quitting. For reasons that have never been fully explained, Jesse Elliott, Perry's temperamental second-in-command, had stayed out of the battle. Oddly, this inexplicable dereliction of duty had a positive side. It meant that Perry had a second seaworthy brig, *Niagara*, in which to fight on. He called for a boat to row him across the turbulent water, and with British round shot splashing about him, he managed to reach *Niagara* and take command.

Barclay, back on deck after his wound was dressed, saw *Niagara* bearing down on him. At that moment a charge of American grapeshot tore his shoulder blade to pieces. His second-in-command also fell, mortally wounded. A young, inexperienced officer did his best to bring the badly mauled flagship about and in doing so became hopelessly entangled with *Queen Charlotte*.

Perry had no trouble manoeuvring *Niagara* into position. He loosed his broadside, raking the entangled ships. At that point every British commander and every second-in-command was a casualty, unable to remain on deck or direct the fighting. It was all over.

Perry's victory was absolute and unprecedented. It was the first time in history that an entire British fleet had been defeated and captured by its adversary. The ships built on the banks of a wilderness lake had served their purpose. They would not fight again.

Erie was now an American lake, guarding the American advance up the Thames River. Detroit and the surrounding American territories, which had been in British hands since the previous year, were abandoned. Lake Ontario remained a kind of watery no-man's-land.

The British clung to the strategic island of Mackinac. The Americans tried to recapture it and failed. That ended the war on the far northern lakes. Lake Huron remained an English sea, and the fur country as far south as St. Louis stayed under British control and would do so until diplomatic horse trading in far-off Ghent restored the status quo. In those negotiations both sides tried to argue that they should "own" the lakes. The British government "considered the lakes from Lake Ontario to Lake Superior . . . to be the natural military frontier of the British possessions in North America." If the Americans gained command of the lakes, as they certainly wanted to, that "would afford the American government the means of commencing a war in the heart of Canada." The Americans would have none of this. But both sides were so weary of the war, unable to agree about the ownership of the inland seas, that they turned the matter over to a number of boundary commissions, where cooler heads prevailed. As Michael F. Scheuer has written: "Each nation's desire to 'own' the Great Lakes was ultimately translated . . . into a shared realization that the Great Lakes–St. Lawrence waterway was the common heritage of both." Thus everything remained as it had been on the Great Lakes when this foolish war began.

Or did it? We can see now that major conflicts have a way of defining the historical boundary lines between two periods. This totally unnecessary but very bloody war marked a significant transition in the story of the lakes. The native tribes who had done so much to frustrate the Americans' efforts were given short shrift. Soon they would be banished to government-controlled reservations. The age of the voyageur was nearly over, too. The lakes no longer echoed to their songs. The era of the settler was dawning, a period that would see the great pine forests vanish with the beaver, that would bring a series of gaudy mining rushes to the hinterland, and that would create a network of canals to transform the character of the great water highway.

The whole contest smacks of the ridiculous—fifteen wooden sailing ships, blasting away at each other in the heart of a wilderness lake, five hundred crow's-flight miles from saltwater.

CHAPTER FIVE

THE ONTONAGON BOULDER AND OTHER TALES OF TREASURE

The great copper rush, inspired by the Ontonagon Boulder, led to the eventual discovery of iron in the hills of Minnesota. This moon-like expanse is not the result of nature's ravages; it is the work of modern machinery, which has gnawed out a vast open pit in the rich Mesabi Range.

THE HISTORY OF MINING STAMPEDES, AS I WELL KNOW, IS REPLETE WITH QUIRKY sagas and bizarre footnotes. Julius Eldred's quest for the Ontanagon Boulder fits neatly into the genre—one of a long series of tales of high hopes and shattered dreams.

Eldred wanted the Ontanagon Boulder in the worst way. He didn't just want it; he was obsessed by it. The miracle rock, so he was told, lay on the muddy bank of the Ontanagon River, some thirty miles from the point where it enters Lake Superior.

It was no ordinary boulder. It was said to weigh at least three tons, maybe four, and it was solid copper—not copper ore, but copper—all the way through. An acquaintance, Joseph Spencer, had seen it twenty years before, shining brilliantly in the sunshine during an expedition with the governor of Michigan Territory, Lewis Cass. His description made Eldred's mouth water. He didn't want to sell the boulder for its copper or chop it into trinkets. He wanted to exhibit it. This, after all, was the age of P.T. Barnum. If people were willing to pay to see Tom Thumb or the Siamese Twins, surely they would shell out a quarter apiece to view the legendary boulder from the Keweenaw Peninsula.

The tale of the great boulder, hidden away in the wilderness, had whetted the public's imagination. Alexander Henry the Elder, fur trader and explorer, had been the first white man to see it—had even managed to chop off a hundred-pound chip as a souvenir. Even then the boulder was scarred by the axes and knives of those aboriginal visitors who had made a pilgrimage to see it. The Ojibwa Indians revered the boulder, believing it to be protected by a powerful manitou. In 1820 six members of the Cass expedition had set out to find it, guided by a luckless tribesman named White Bird who managed first to get Governor Cass lost in the bush (Cass never did see the boulder) and then to get himself banished by his tribe for defying a sacred taboo.

Now, in 1841, taboo or no taboo, Julius Eldred, a tall, swarthy Detroit hardware merchant with an eye for opportunity, decided to make the boulder his own.

Nobody yet realized that the Keweenaw Peninsula of Michigan, which juts out into Lake Superior like an outstretched thumb, was a treasure trove of solid copper. The scientists of that day did not believe that copper could be found in its pure state but only as copper ore. The Keweenaw was the exception. It was one of the rare corners of the globe where pure copper could be found and mined, a fact long known to the Indians.

Eldred made his way from Detroit to the Ontanagon and without much trouble found the boulder on Indian land. It wasn't hard to spot. There it lay, close to the river, gleaming in the sun. He paid the local chief one hundred and fifty dollars and made plans to get it out to civilization—no easy task. Since the mass was so unwieldy, however, he didn't think anyone else would try to move it.

He was back in the summer of 1843 with a crew of twenty-one men, block and tackle, a flatcar, and several yards of railroad track. Only then did he find that a group of Wisconsin miners was on the scene, surrounding the boulder and claiming it as their own. Eldred didn't want trouble, but he did want the boulder and was willing to pay these entrepreneurs $1,365 for it. He hoisted it onto the flatcar, which rolled down the short bit of track. By leap-frogging the track he managed to get his prize over hills, swamps, and forests to the main course of the river, where it could be floated by barge to the lake. He had also had the foresight to secure a permit from the local mineral agent to move it.

At the Detroit docks, Eldred was welcomed by a forty-piece band. A triumphal procession followed, with the boulder in a wagon drawn by four black stallions. Eldred was in business—or thought he was. But, just as the townspeople were queuing up to see the miracle rock, Washington stepped in

The photograph below, made in 1924 at Hibbing, Minnesota, shows how the Mesabi was stripped of its treasure. More than seventy years later the process still continues, albeit for a lower-grade ore.

and overruled its own mineral agent. The boulder had become so famous that it must be put on display in the nation's capital. It was moved to the Smithsonian Institution, where the bureaucrats forgot about it. It took more than four years of legal wrangling before Eldred got compensation for his expenses (or some of them): $5,664.90 in total. He died in 1851, a much disillusioned man.

The boulder, which was eventually moved to the Museum of Natural History, can be seen today, a symbol of the richness of the Lake Superior copper country—and the stampede it caused. In 1843, after the state geologist, Douglass Houghton, reported that in a single explosion he had detached a forty-pound chunk of pure copper from a surface outcropping, the rush was on.

Large masses of pure copper, like this one photographed in the shaft of the Quincy Mine on Lake Superior's Keweenaw Peninsula, were almost unknown elsewhere. By the 1920s Quincy miners were working more than a mile below the surface.

The Keweenaw Peninsula wasn't easy to reach, but great mineral finds never are. That has always added to the romance of mining stampedes. That eloquent American, Patrick Henry, said that the Keweenaw was "beyond the most distant wilderness and remote as the moon." So, of course, was California in '49 and the Klondike in '98. To reach the copper country the stampeders had to travel to Sault Ste Marie in Canada and then brave one hundred and fifty miles of turbulent Lake Superior water.

None of that deterred the thundering herd. I am reminded of my own father heading up the Stikine River, trying vainly to reach the goldfields by that route, which by then was a heaving and impassable swamp. Did he abandon the quest? Hardly; he changed direction, then pushed on to the very base of the Chilkoot Pass, where a letter was awaiting him offering the sinecure of a teaching job at Queen's. He didn't take it. The lure of precious metal or perhaps the adventure of it all drove him on. He shouldered his sixty-pound pack and prepared to climb and re-climb the Pass more than thirty times to get his ton of goods past the Mounties at the summit.

The stampeders who reached the Sault in search of copper were of the same mettle. Too impatient to wait for a proper boat, they engaged French-Canadians to brave the fury of the lake in flimsy birch-bark canoes. Soon the booming peninsula was throbbing with the usual cluster of saloons, bawdy houses, and dance halls that accompany every stampede. As one scandalized

Detroit newspaperman wrote, ". . . there's no such day as the Sabbath, west of Sault Ste Marie."

As I well know, every mining rush creates its own legends, sturdy enough to stimulate the newcomers to further exertions. The copper boom was no exception. One mine at Copper Falls owed its existence, so it was said, to the thirst of a prospector who bent over Owl Creek, seeking a cooling drink, and saw a seam of water-polished copper gleaming under the rippling surface. The Cliff Mine, the most fabulous on the peninsula, was discovered literally by accident when a prospector slipped down the face of a greenstone cliff and was caught on a projection of solid copper. The Cliff, which opened in 1845, was the world's richest copper mine. During its life it produced thirty-eight million pounds of native copper, paid dividends for thirty-five years, and rewarded its original investors with a return of 2,000 percent on their money.

In the winter of 1846, Samuel O. Knapp noticed a depression under the snow, examined it, and routed several porcupine from their hibernating cavern. In the cave he discovered a trove of ancient stone hammers and another boulder of pure copper weighing sixty tons, resting on a cribbing of rotting logs. Before he could reach the bottom of the ancient mine he had removed ten loads of hammers, one weighing almost forty pounds. And there, at the bottom, was a vein of pure copper, five feet wide. A hemlock growing in the property showed 395 rings, meaning that the tree had already reached maturity and the natives were working in the mines in Columbus's day. This odd discovery of ancient native diggings was the genesis of the great Minesota mine, whose shaft had been driven directly through an enormous mass of solid metal. Thus, for some distance, the walls of the Minesota shaft were of solid copper. Nobody cared that the name was misspelled.

The development of electricity brought new uses for copper. As the price went up, the shafts went down. By the end of the century the Calumet and Hecla Mining Company distributed ten million dollars in dividends in a single year. The Great War increased the demand, and when the Roaring Twenties arrived, the engineers of the Quincy Mine astonished the world by sinking a shaft sixty-five-hundred feet into the bowels of the earth. Only in the diamond mines of Kimberley had anyone gone deeper. It was a final gesture. When the Great Depression struck, the market began to decline and the price of copper plummeted to a nickel a pound. Today there is no copper left on the Keweenaw Peninsula.

These tales of rich strikes on Superior's rim are intertwined. Men seeking

FACING PAGE: **Posed against the rocky face of the great open pit at the Mesabi, the miners of another era stare resolutely at the camera.**

one precious metal stumbled upon another. It was surely no accident that Douglass Houghton, the state geologist who helped touch off the copper boom in the early 1840s, also helped launch the iron fever. On September 19, 1844, some of his crew noticed that their compass needles were going crazy on an outcropping eighty miles southeast of Keweenaw. Here they found chunks of pure iron. That was the clue that led to the discovery of the largest and richest deposits of iron ore in the world.

Six great ridges of iron encircle the lake. In the quarter century following Houghton's original find, they were uncovered one by one. Houghton's men had stumbled upon the vast Marquette Range. Thirty years would pass before its neighbour, the Menominee, was explored.

In the interval there were other finds. In 1865 two reconnaissance surveyors, Richard and Harry Eames, found a bed of hard iron near Vermilion Lake in Minnesota not far from the Canadian border. They also found specimens of iron pyrites, "fool's gold," which they mistook for the real thing. It didn't matter. As always, the magic word "gold" touched off a stampede to Vermilion Lake.

There are elements of irony in every mining stampede. Hundreds of men were tramping through the forest tangle seeking gold while lurking beneath their boots were the two greatest iron deposits in the world—the Vermilion and Mesabi ranges.

George Stuntz was one of these, but he was also an amateur geologist, tough, wiry, and shrewd. He was not fooled by fool's gold; he knew iron when he saw it. He was convinced that a mountain of it lay waiting to be uncovered in the Vermilion country. The range was only fifteen miles long—the oldest, geologically, of all the iron mountains—but its high-quality ore went as deep as two thousand feet. It took twenty years and a huge investment to bring in a mine. But over the next quarter century it produced thirty million tons.

These stories of mining ventures around the lakes have two things in common: they are all similar and they are all endlessly fascinating. They deal with greed and adversity; with fortunes won and squandered; with triumph and failure; with blind luck and dogged persistence; with opportunities lost; and with hidden wealth ignored. The story of the Mesabi is no exception.

This range consists of a series of granite-topped hills worn down over time. Seven million years ago it lay submerged beneath a vast inland sea over whose floor successive lava flows built up into a blanket seven thousand feet thick. That was the beginning of the Mesabi Range, changed and deformed

first by the heaving up of the land, then by the erosion of wind and water, and finally by the scraping and gouging of the ice sheets.

Here was the greatest concentration of iron ore so far discovered in all the world, but the Minesota Iron Company, working the neighbouring Vermilion, missed it. Even though the company built a railroad directly across the Mesabi's eastern end, it didn't cotton on to the wealth in the surrounding rocks. The presence of iron in the Mesabi had been known since 1875, but the experts who examined it didn't think it was worth bothering about. They didn't understand the structure—didn't know that the iron was overlain with glacial drift, a few inches in some places, a hundred feet in others. The outcrop rocks they thought "too thin," but just below there lay concealed what one historian of the Mesabi, Harland Hatcher, has called "an iron man's dream of the inconceivable."

Hardly anyone believed in the Mesabi. The five Merritt brothers, sons of a prolific Duluth timber cruiser, were exceptions. In 1887, one of them, Cassius, discovered a boulder of high-grade, Bessemer-quality ore. This convinced the brothers, in spite of the experts' adverse reports, that there was iron in the Mesabi. The banks, of course, believed the experts and advanced only limited credit. The brothers persevered nonetheless, buying up land and leases and sinking test holes. Always the iron eluded them. At one point they were a few feet from their goal. The test hole was on the very edge of the range, but it produced nothing.

They kept on. On November 16, 1890, they found a deposit that looked like red sand some twelve feet beneath the surface. That was another disappointment, but they tested it anyway. To their delight it contained 90 percent pure iron ore. This find was in the very heart of the yet-to-be-surveyed range, and it suggested that much of Mesabi's iron ore didn't have to be blasted from the earth. It could be scooped up with gigantic shovels.

Even then the experts were dubious. Andrew Carnegie, the steel king, refused to back the Merritts in spite of the mad scramble for leases that took place in the mid-nineties. Yet in the end, the great range, shaped like a monstrous serpent one hundred miles long and never more than two miles wide, would produce more iron than all the other ranges put together. The open pit at Hibbing, three miles across and 435 feet deep, sprawls over 1,250 acres.

It would be pleasant to report that the Merritt brothers profited from all this, but they didn't. They were outfoxed by John D. Rockefeller, and after a series of court battles they settled privately for a small undisclosed sum and vanished from the scene. Overshadowed in the mid-twentieth century by the discoveries in Labrador, the Mesabi Range declined but did not expire. The Labrador operation has been closed, but the Mesabi still produces. It yields low-grade ore now. The glory days are over.

About the same time that the Eames brothers were locating iron near Vermilion Lake, two other surveyors were setting up their transits on a nameless reef in Lake Superior. They had been enticed there in the summer of 1868 by reports that the copper deposits on the Keweenaw Peninsula across the lake might have reappeared on the north shore. In order to find a level setting for their transit they chipped away with a crowbar at a piece of rock on the shore and found it veined with a greyish white metal. Part of the rock was submerged, and under the rippling water they could see the vein continue, widening to two feet. Polished by the action of the water, it shone like a silver dollar. Silver!

Thus began the saga of Silver Islet, a Canadian phenomenon that one historian has called "the most remarkable silver mine the world has ever known." Here on a speck of rock no more than eight feet above the storm-tossed lake and no bigger than a baseball diamond was a sultan's ransom in silver. The richness of this half-submerged island was almost unbelievable. Mining men were still talking in hushed tones about the riches of Nevada's Comstock Lode, discovered nine years before. Comstock ore had assayed at a remarkable three thousand ounces a ton. But at its peak, Silver Islet's ore would assay at an incredible 17,000 ounces a ton.

The Montreal Mining Company, which employed the two surveyors, had no stomach for digging into a bit of submerged reef at the far end of an unexplored lake. The cautious Canadians sold the islet for a quarter of a million dollars to a more adventurous syndicate of Michigan mining men and thought themselves well rid of it. Perhaps they were.

Out to Silver Islet in May 1870 came the syndicate's company manager, a raw-boned redhead named William Bell Frue, who is the real hero of the Silver Islet saga. Frue realized that it would be impossible to mine this storm-buffeted bit of rock until it was made secure from the ravages of the lake. Accordingly, he encircled it with a two-hundred-foot breakwater, the logs secured with heavy steel bolts, while the islet's main shaft was protected by a cofferdam. None of this did any good. The lake became Frue's nemesis and

The tales of rich strikes on Superior's rim are intertwined. Men seeking one precious metal stumbled upon another. It was surely no accident that the geologist who touched off the copper boom also helped launch the iron fever.

would continue to be so for the next five years. The breakwater was scarcely in place before it was destroyed by the lash of waves that swept away a two-hundred-foot length, tossing the logs about like matchwood and twisting the ten-inch bolts like rubber tubing. "My wife's hairpins would have done as much good," said Frue, ruefully.

Frue and his crew set to work at once to repair the damage, building a double wall of cribbing and filling it with rocks. In the four weeks left to him before winter closed in, his team raised ore worth more than one hundred thousand dollars. When the assay figures reached the outside world with the last shipment, the stock market went crazy. Shares that couldn't sell earlier at one hundred dollars were now being snapped up at five thousand. Then a December storm sealed the entire islet in ice and dispersed a gigantic boom containing twenty thousand feet of squared logs. There wasn't enough timber left to construct a new bulwark. Frue fought on, promising to reward the first man who could find a grove of white pine large enough to replace the missing timber.

By March the big trees that the winner discovered were cut and the logs bolted into place. But the lake waters again engulfed the islet, once more battering the wooden barriers with tons of ice, leaving the work in ruins.

Storm after storm hit the island, smashing Frue's repairs as quickly as he made them. In November 1873, the worst storm of all—"a real gagger," in Frue's words—swept over the islet. "All previous storms were dwarfed," Frue reported. "They were mere zephyrs compared with the hurricane that now swept down from the northeast." Clinging to the top of the cofferdam, Frue watched as a sixty-foot stretch of cribbing toppled and a Niagara of water poured down upon him. A boiler exploded, killing two of his men, and a piece of falling debris knocked Frue into the water-filled cofferdam. A

Silver Islet, looking south, as it appeared in 1921 after a Duluth firm took over and attempted to make it pay. The cost of the venture far exceeded the rewards, and the mine closed. Today, as the waters wash over the silver reef, there is no remaining sign of human presence. The lake has won the battle.

huge wave slammed him against the shaft house. He clung to a protruding beam until the waters receded.

The breakwater was again in ruins: twenty thousand additional feet of timber lost along with seven and a half tons of bolts, while five tons of rocks "were whirled around the Islet like hailstones."

In spite of these delays the mine kept shipping high-grade silver. But the company had had enough. It was prepared to pocket the considerable profits and quit. The indefatigable Frue, however, would have none of that. His newest plan was to increase the islet's size by dumping rock around the edges.

By this time several hundred people were living at the landing across from Silver Islet, while several buildings, including four log boardinghouses, had been built on the islet itself. Then, unexpectedly, in 1875 Frue left the job. No one knew why, but it is possible to speculate that in the end Lake Superior was too much for him.

Under a new manager, production reached its peak. "Silver of unparalleled richness" was found. After that, production went into a decline. The main shaft was down to 1,200 feet—an expensive depth. To keep it from flooding, the company had to keep steam-driven pumps running continually. To keep fires going to produce the steam, an extraordinary amount of coal was needed. A shipload of coal was ordered, but once again the lake won out. The ship was locked in the ice, and the men on Silver Islet were reduced to ripping apart buildings to feed the boilers.

In March the fuel ran out, and as the pumps slowed to a halt, the mine began to fill with water. The company did not choose to reopen it. In 1920, a Duluth firm made a faltering attempt to mine more silver ore, but the cost of mining far exceeded the value of the silver. And that was the end of Silver Islet.

The silver is still there, of course. The mine's roof is almost solid silver ore, and so are the heavy pillars left to support it. It makes a marvellous fantasy—the kind you read about in children's fairy-tale books. Here, hidden deep below the sullen waters of a great lake, lies a silver room with a silver roof, supported by silver pillars. But no prince in disguise can enter the room to carry off its glittering treasure, for if he does, the unsupported roof will tumble, sealing him forever in a silver grave.

Romantic though it is, the saga of Silver Islet pales before that of the Hemlo gold discovery, not far from the town of Marathon on Lake Superior's north shore. Of all the gold finds in the Superior region, this was the biggest. The block of gold-bearing ore at Hemlo is estimated to be worth some ten *billion* dollars. Yet a century went by between discovery and exploitation. Though the first prospectors found gold in the ores of the area just one year after the discovery of Silver Islet, Hemlo did not begin to produce gold until 1985.

The story of the Hemlo find—a gigantic mother lode a mile square and a mile deep—is yet another tangled tale of sheer blind luck, of chances missed, of fortunes discarded, and of millions made overnight. It covers more than a century of lost opportunities and shrewd gambles. It begins in 1869 when a native, Moses Pe-Kong-Gay, located the first gold. Shafts were sunk and ore shipped, but the trouble that every prospector and prospective mine owner faced was the quality of the ore and the prevailing price of gold. The quality was too poor; a ton of ore yielded less than a quarter ounce of gold. Only when gold began to stabilize above four hundred dollars an ounce was mining low-grade ore profitable.

Nor did anybody actually find the real body of ore that many years later would turn some men into millionaires. In the 1920s experienced prospectors were trenching and drilling right through the heart of the Hemlo field and finding nothing worthwhile. Decade after decade, optimistic entrepreneurs tested the ground in the Hemlo area but missed the treasure in the rocks.

One man who didn't miss was another native prospector, Peter Moses, who discovered what proved to be the richest ground in the Hemlo district. He persuaded a Maryland physician and amateur gold geologist, Dr. J.K. Williams, to stake eleven claims. Williams managed to get outright title to this ground, known as the Williams Option, which became family property. But he was in no hurry to develop it, perhaps because nobody else could move in and legally stake it. The day would come when it would benefit his widow. Meanwhile, with Peter Moses and several others, Williams did stake some neighbouring ground and formed a company to map, trench, and drill it. They came within a whisker of hitting the now famous Hemlo ore body, but they missed it and gave up. I am reminded of similar tales in my own background.

The property began to change hands. In 1951 Teck Hughes Gold Mines optioned it, drilled down six thousand feet, located eighty-nine thousand tons of low-grade ore, and abandoned it. With gold at thirty-five dollars an ounce,

The photographer who made this picture described these Mesabi range miners as "typical" —a word that photographers use, and often misuse.

mining it just wasn't profitable. The same property was successively staked four times by various prospectors, none of whom could raise a dime to exploit it.

The Trans-Canada Highway ran right past the future Hemlo goldfields. Prospectors came and went on foot, by boat, by car—but the gold remained hidden. Matthew Hart, the chronicler of the Hemlo field, has pointed out how close the gold was to the highway. "You could have stopped your car, walked over to a rock cut, chipped a few pounds off, and stuck it in the trunk."

Still another company staked the ground, sank three holes, and gave up. It was staked again with the same results. But gold prices had risen, and when that ground became available again in December 1979, Don McKinnon, who was waiting for just that moment, pounced.

McKinnon, a bespectacled, scholarly looking fifty-year-old prospector, had researched the history of Hemlo carefully. A Grade 10 dropout, he had studied geology while working for a logging company. He had been waiting a decade for the claims to lapse. He rushed to the spot, staked twelve claims, and ran into his former partner, John Larche, another high school dropout who had come to Hemlo with the same idea. Larche and his son had staked seven claims, and now the two ex-partners decided to join forces again. Next day, the new partnership staked seven more.

The following March they decided to stake six additional claims around those original seven. But when Larche noted that this made a total of thirteen on that part of the property—an unlucky number to him—he suggested they stake another one. The claim, it later developed, was in the very heart of what came to be the Golden Giant, site of the richest ore in the district. Matthew Hart has estimated that ownership of that single claim would bring an income of five hundred dollars every day of the year for twenty years.

The two men raised enough money to finance a staking binge. Within a year they controlled hundreds of thousands of acres in the region. Unable to get as much as a nickel from the cautious Bay Street promoters, they went to Vancouver with its high, wide, and handsome stock exchange. There, the most flamboyant promoter in town, Murray Pezim, backed them, formed a company called Corona Resources, and in the winter of 1980-81 brought in a geologist, David Bell, to oversee the drilling program. Bell has since been hailed as the real discoverer of the Hemlo goldfield.

He endured heartbreaking disappointments. Drill hole after drill hole proved worthless; seventy holes on the western zone of the field came up with nothing. Yet Murray the Pez and his partner, Neil Dragonian, kept pouring in cash.

To most prospectors, Hemlo had always been disappointing. All the gold discovered in Ontario to that time had been found in thin veins of quartz. But Bell had a theory about Hemlo gold. The geology, he realized, was quite different here. There was no quartz, only a thick slab of rock whose upper layer had been metamorphosed from silt and sand and whose lower layer came from ancient deposits of volcanic ash. Bell figured that gold was the ham in this sandwich. He now decided to drill into the dark volcanic rock on the eastern edge of the zone. The first hole, No. 71, showed nothing. The next four holes also came up blank. But hole No. 76 was phenomenal. Here the drills bit into the richest ore in the history of Canadian gold mining.

That made it the most important hole ever drilled in Canada. As Hart has explained, it revolutionized prospecting in Canada. If gold is to be found in volcanic rock as well as in quartz, the entire Canadian Shield is once again up for grabs. By the end of that year, Corona stock was trading at thirty-five dollars a share, and Don McKinnon and John Larche were each worth five million dollars just to begin with.

Now, as the usual frenzied staking rush got underway in the early months of 1981, the spotlight was focused on the Williams Option of fifteen claims. Williams had tied up staking rights in perpetuity, but he had since died and his widow, Lola, wanted to sell. Both Murray Pezim's Corona Resources and the more powerful Lac Minerals pressured her to sell it. Lola chose the stronger company, even though Corona's offer was twice as sweet. Lac paid her a quarter of a million dollars and a future royalty of 1.5 percent on the smelter production—a contract that would pay her almost three million dollars.

Murray the Pez moved in and sued Lac on the grounds that it had misused confidential information. After an eight-year wrangle in the courts, Lac lost and was forced to surrender the property to Corona. On that basis Corona became the largest gold producer in Canada and one of the three largest in North America. By then, of course, Hemlo was an established field and Murray the Pez had been eased out of control. It was the quest that had driven him on—not the reward.

The Trans-Canada Highway ran right past the future Hemlo goldfields. Prospectors came and went—but the gold remained hidden. Yet it was so close you could have stopped your car, walked over to a rock cut, and chipped a few pounds off.

Ghostly memories of a vanished era

The remains of once-lively mining towns litter the Lake Superior hinterland to remind us that the boom rarely lasts.

Most of the photographs on these pages were taken at Fayette Historical Townsite, Michigan. Here, half hidden by the encroaching foliage, are reminders of the raucous days when these streets echoed to the sounds of thirsty miners heading for the saloons.

At the ghost town of Delaware, Michigan, these crumbling structures, like the one at Fayette (OPPOSITE), take me back to my Yukon days, when, in the post-gold rush era, roadhouse saloons and cabins rotted away among the birches and cottonwoods.

OVERLEAF: The skeleton of the once-thriving ore dock at Michipicoten Bay on the northeastern shore of Lake Superior recalls the days when lake freighters were moored here with ore for eastern smelters.

CHAPTER SIX

THE DEATH OF
THE LAKE FORESTS

The largest load of lumber ever hauled on a sleigh was loaded at Ewen, Michigan, February 26, 1893. It was destined for the Michigan exhibit at the World's Columbian Exposition in Chicago where wide-eyed thousands viewed it.

PREVIOUS PAGES: This forest at Hartwick, Michigan, is a museum piece—one of the last stands of the white pines that once surrounded the lakes in the millions.

W E CANNOT COMPREHEND TODAY THE EXTENT OF THE GREAT PINE FOREST that rimmed the upper lakes in the early nineteenth century. To say that there were millions of trees—millions upon millions upon millions—does not convey the awesome nature of this wealth of timberland. The forest seemed eternal, or so our forefathers believed. In 1852 a Wisconsin congressman spoke publicly of "interminable forests of pine sufficient to supply all the wants of the citizens . . . *for all time to come*" [my emphasis].

Yet all this was destroyed in little more than fifty years.

At mid-century that was inconceivable. "Trees, trees, trees for everlasting," wrote Frederick Graham in his diary as he accompanied Sir George Simpson beyond Lake Superior. "I shall hate the sight of a wood for the future." To the early explorers and the first settlers, this vast ocean of conifers reaching beyond the far horizons was more than awe inspiring. It was a little terrifying.

Conrad Richter caught it in his novel *The Trees*: ". . . they looked down on . . . a dark, illimitable expanse of wilderness. It was a sea of solid treetops broken only by some gash where deep beneath the foliage an unknown stream made its way. As far as the eye could reach, this lonely forest sea rolled on and on till its faint blue billows broke against an incredibly distant horizon. . . ."

Yet by the end of the century the slaughter of the pines was all but over. By 1897 the forest surrounding the lakes had been destroyed by what is now known as the Big Cut.

Somebody has figured out that enough white pine was cut by the Great Lakes states to build ten million six-room houses, or to build fifty-one plank roads, each fifty feet wide and an inch thick, from New York to San Francisco. The figures for the north shore of Georgian Bay are comparable. This was big business and the statistics are astonishing. For instance, the total value of the lumber produced in Michigan exceeded the value of gold production in California by one billion dollars.

Today it is fashionable to look back and condemn those who so ruthlessly savaged the legacy of the past. But we can afford the luxury of an enlightened attitude now. The crusade to save the forests, whether it targets British Columbia or Brazil, has been growing over the past generation. I myself was recently involved in the battle to preserve the old-growth forest of Clayoquot Sound on Vancouver Island. This is all well and proper in the context of the late twentieth century, when we have less need for lumber than our forefathers had, but I do not believe that I would have addressed mass rallies to save the white pine of the Great Lakes, even if such rallies had been held.

We must remember that there was a time when the dark, mysterious forest world—the wilderness—was seen as an enemy to be conquered. Folk memories die hard. The forests of fantasy were peopled with wolves, bears, witches, and all manner of strange and terrible creatures. The age-old tale of Red Riding Hood, in its many versions, was part of the cultural baggage of the day. And there was more to it than fear of the unknown. Clearing the land, chopping down the trees, blasting the stumps, and tilling the soil was a form of progress to which every pioneer owed a duty. My schoolbooks were larded with praise for such stalwarts.

"Filling up the plains" was part of John A. Macdonald's National Policy following the construction of the Pacific Railway. It must be remembered that there was hardly a stick of wood to be found on the southern prairie and its U.S. counterpart at that time. The first settlers were reduced to creating hovels out of the tough western turf. It was the white-pine forests of the Great Lakes that made possible decent housing for the settlers of the western plains.

I was raised in a northern community that depended entirely on wood. We had no brick, no stone, no cement. Every house was built of boards or logs. The very sidewalks on which we made our way to school were wooden. And there was no coal. In our stoves and furnaces we burned birch wood cut from the hills above town. Long stacks of neatly piled logs stretched away behind the Administration Building where my father worked. Along the river at designated spots were more stacks to operate the steamboats that plied the river. The Klondike hills had long since been denuded of trees to fuel the boilers that supplied steam to thaw the valleys where the gold lay hidden. The entire Northwest depended on wood, and to a large extent still does.

For these reasons I can understand the role that wood played in pioneer North America. It was to the nineteenth century what petroleum has been to the twentieth. Every man, woman, and child in North America used an average of three hundred and fifty board feet a year. Wood products entered into every aspect of life. Almost every structure—houses, barns, warehouses, mills, railway stations, factories—was built of wood. Everybody

OVERLEAF: When the ice broke in the early spring, thousands of logs hurtled down the Muskegon River to the mills on Lake Michigan. The logs were guided by workmen with tools known as peavies. It was hard, dangerous work.

from carriage maker to cooper used wood. In the countryside it was the principal source of fencing. Wood charcoal was the essential ingredient in the manufacture of pig iron. Wood was also the major household fuel and the key to the transportation system.

One single statistic highlights the voracious demand for wood in the last century. In the late 1880s there were in North America some 160,000 miles of railway track. Each mile of track required 2,500 eight-foot railway ties. Before the introduction of creosote, no tie lasted more than ten years. No forest, no matter how vast, could withstand this constant drain.

More than any other tree, the white pine, the giant of the forest, was ideal for the needs of the day. It was light, strong, and durable. It did not warp, crack, shrink, or splinter. The mature trees rose to a height of one hundred and fifty feet; some had been seedlings in Columbus's day. Their trunks were at least four feet in diameter, and since they lost their lower branches in the first fifty feet of growth, the lumber they produced was free of knots. Conditions around the lakes were perfect for pine. They even flourished on the sandy soils. The climate, which was itself controlled by the presence of vast sheets of water, fitted them. And they had one great asset: they could float!

Entire forests toppled into the water, the logs borne lightly on the frothing streams to the mills at their mouths or to the lakes themselves, where they could be towed in vast booms to the larger centres. Chicago, at the foot of Lake Michigan, was built on the lumber trade. By the 1850s it had become the greatest lumber market in the world. "In no other city on the planet," the city's biographer, William Cronon, has written, "was there a neighborhood to compare with the vast, strange landscape of stacked wood that dominated the South Branch of the Chicago River." The endless heaps of lumber, piled ten feet high, stretched as far as the eye could see. Here, where lumber was turned into hard cash, a city within a city sprang up. The docks that nurtured the lumber ships ran for twelve miles along the river.

It was an age of superlatives. Bigness was worshipped for its own sake as it sometimes is today. In 1872, the *Antelope*, one of seven hundred steamers and clippers in the Great Lakes lumber trade, towed the biggest footage in history into Buffalo. Eight vast barges made a mile-long procession, "as large a navy as Perry commanded in Put-In Bay." In February 1893, a group of lumberjacks in northern Michigan managed to create for the Columbian Exposition the largest single load of logs in history. Each log was eighteen feet long, and the load itself was thirty feet high and sixteen feet wide. A single team of horses hauled the load out of the woods, but it required nine railway flatcars to move this "World's Fair Load" from the shipping point to Chicago.

For the lumber barons it was an age of extravagance. "No mortal could possibly know how much I spent," the impeccably tailored A.G.P. "Alphabet" Dodge remarked ruefully after his bankruptcy in the late seventies. The scion of a wealthy American business and professional family, Dodge moved to Canada to found the huge Georgian Bay Lumber Company, whose timber limits reached out from Collingwood to Blind River, Ontario. Next to the Ottawa Valley's legendary J.R. Booth, Dodge was Canada's biggest lumber king. He didn't need to take a salary because the company paid all his personal expenses, from his vast, 220-acre estate, Beechcroft, on Lake Simcoe right down to the pet deer he kept in the park and to the solid-gold cuff links and scarf rings that were a symbol of the period.

Alphabet Dodge went gloriously broke, was bailed out by his father, and was succeeded by his younger brother, Arthur, who was just as profligate. Arthur Dodge constructed an even more lavish mansion at Waubaushene, raised herds of prize cattle and sheep, and cruised about Georgian Bay in his *Skylark*, "the most elegant yacht afloat."

The company survived these extravagances, but it could not survive the Big Cut. By the early 1900s, technological advances had made it possible to strip a thirty-six-mile timber berth clear of pine in just ten years. Even Arthur Dodge's penny-pinching successor, W.J. Sheppard, a one-time timber scaler, couldn't save it. By the 1920s the company was effectively out of business.

Robert Dollar, the Scottish-born lumberman who got his start in the camboose camps of Georgian Bay and the Ottawa Valley, saw which way the wind was blowing. Dollar moved to Michigan, where the logs were larger, worked as a lumberjack, founded the mill town of Dollarville, and then, having made his first fortune in just five years, decamped to California before the trees ran out. With his profits he founded the round-the-world Dollar Line to become the largest individual shipowner in the United States.

Canadian loggers, mainly Quebeckers (the so-called red sash brigade), streamed across the border through Sarnia to work in the Michigan camps, where the wages were higher. By 1880, forty thousand Canadians were logging in the Lakes states. In spite of the ebb and flow, Canada was losing seven thousand loggers a year—men like the notorious T.C. Cunnion, who wore a stiff

In Chicago, the endless heaps of lumber, piled ten feet high, stretched as far as the eye could see. Here, where lumber was turned into hard cash, a city within a city sprang up. The docks that nurtured the lumber ships ran for twelve miles along the river.

boiled shirt under his mackinaw and burst into the Saginaw saloons, bawling out that he was "the maneater from Peterborough, Ontario." He liked to roar into butcher shops, seize a lump of liver, and eat it raw; but he was brought down when a woman entering a shop spotted the maneater with blood all over his face, screamed, and felled him with a single blow of her umbrella. After that humiliation, the Peterborough Maneater left Saginaw forever.

It could not have happened in Canada, for there is a contrast in national styles. The mill towns that flourished on both sides of the border—Waubaushene, Penetanguishene, Collingwood, and Parry Sound in Canada, Saginaw, Muskegon, Bay City, and others in the United States—underline that contrast. North of the border temperance reigned. Any employee of the Georgian Bay Lumber Company was instantly dismissed if the slightest whiff of the demon rum sullied his breath. In Waubaushene, known for its "thrift, beauty, and lumbering business," the leading caravansary was the thirty-six-room Donkin House, named, significantly, for the man who wrote the Canada Temperance Act of 1864. The Orillia *Times* in 1884 praised "the health and happiness of those whose privilege it was to have a home . . . in the charming village of Waubaushene." When Arthur Dodge announced boldly that the public reading room of the local library would actually be opened on Sunday, there was a public furore from those who believed "the Sabbath should be kept inviolate."

As Waubaushene went, so did the neighbouring communities. In his history of the Georgian Bay Lumber Company, James T. Angus has noted how "the puritanical cement poured into the commercial framework by the founders was too strong to allow social decay. Temperance was still the order of the day . . . the Protestant work ethic and the stern, uncompromising creed of the dominant Presbyterian congregation continued to determine the mores and create the social sanctions that controlled the behaviour of the villagers."

In sharp contrast, the lumber towns of the lower Michigan peninsula rivalled the lawlessness of the Kansas cowtowns. The police and town marshals, who supplied what little law and order existed, were regularly drunk and often corrupt. As a result, citizens formed "Public Safety Committees" of vigilantes in an attempt to enforce the law.

There were exceptions. East Saginaw had its own Wyatt Earp in the person of an ex-cavalryman, Marshal Charles Meyer, who managed to quell the mass donnybrooks in the saloons by riding his horse into the barroom and flailing about with a nightstick. Muskegon's Patrick Ryan was another tough officer. He once allowed a drunken lumberjack to get off six shots at him without returning the fire. When his adversary's gun was empty, he clubbed him and hauled him off to jail. He hadn't shot back, he said, "because the man was drunk."

The courts were remarkably lenient with lawbreakers. In the Michigan lumber towns, 112 murders were committed over a twenty-year period. Sixty-three of the accused got off scot-free. Only six were imprisoned. The main defence plea was intoxication, and no wonder. On Saginaw's Potter Street, thirty-two saloons were crowded into a distance of nine blocks. And that was on only one side of the street.

Potter Street faced the railway depot. Here it was common to see a train pull in without a single whole pane of glass in any of the ten coaches. Michigan lumber towns vied to be known as the toughest of all. East Saginaw's White Row was called "the roughest, toughest, fightingest spot in the Saginaws." Bay City's Catacombs was "undoubtedly the toughest place anywhere along the Saginaw River." It was said you could smell the booze emanating from Muskegon's famous Sawdust Flats as far away as fifty miles. Here, in six long blocks of "unspeakable whoredom" (to quote a local divine), three hundred prostitutes plied their trade. And here such larger-than-life figures as Spanish Lou, who could curse in eight languages, and Big Delia contributed to local

In 1907, at Split Rock River, Lake Superior, men with peavies tie the floating logs together to form a gigantic raft.

legend. Big Delia—the Big Deal—was a strapping, tobacco-chewing woman who brooked no nonsense from her customers. Once she hit an obstreperous logger so hard she broke his jaw—and her knuckles.

The Sawdust Flats were built on sawdust fill—acres of it, mountains of it. The mills produced hundreds of thousands of tons of this by-product, and nobody knew what to do with it. Usually this waste was dumped into the mill-streams, a practice that sometimes created new islands. As early as 1865, the Oconto River in Wisconsin was said to be paved with sawdust and slabs of rotting bark. Sawdust was difficult to burn as fuel and impossible as a fill because it decayed so quickly. It clogged the river estuaries, forming a thick bottom covering that fanned far out into the coastal waters, obliterating the bottom muck and turning wetlands into deserts. Deprived of their spawning and feeding grounds, such important fish as the Atlantic salmon and the blue pike vanished from the lakes.

The white pine has gone the way of the blue pike. A few demonstration stands, such as the one at Hartwick, Michigan, remain preserved, like the Parthenon, as testimony to the riches of the past. Few voices were raised to protest the rape of these forests. "Progress" had a different context in the nine-teenth century than it has in the twentieth.

And yet one man successfully resisted the combined pressure of private enterprise and government. He was Michel Dokis, leader of a small band of Indians who lived along the French River in the Georgian Bay forest. Every attempt was made to force him to sell the white pine on his sixty-one square miles of reserve. He steadfastly refused to do so. No lumberman, it seemed, could get it into his head that Chief Dokis's band valued the white pine for itself and not for what it would bring in cash.

It is a scandalous story, for the federal government was clearly on the side of the timber interests. It used every tactic—threats, bribery, deception—to force Dokis's band to sell its timber rights. An attempt was even made to change the Indian Act to force the "unreasonable" Indians to sell out. But Dokis and his band stood firm.

One can sense the astonishment in the report of Thomas Walton, the regional superintendent for the Department of Indian Affairs, who was driven to the conclusion that "sentimental rather than monetary considerations" guided the natives' conduct. To love great stands of trees for their own sake was, in short, a mental aberration.

Walton tried to ride roughshod over the Indians' interests. Dokis's conduct, he reported, "exemplifies in a marked degree the incapacity of the Indians to manage their own affairs." As a result, he recommended that the Indian department sell the timber without the natives' consent. Fortunately that proved legally impossible.

The Liberal M.P. for Nipissing now moved in and managed to get a friend appointed Indian agent for the region; he had specific instructions to force the Indians to surrender their timber rights. That could not be done legally. Although all these machinations were cloaked in protestations that it was all for the Indians' own good, it seems obvious that the Indian department was working hand in glove with American and Canadian timber interests who were desperate for this last stand of virgin pine.

Chief Dokis held out for thirty years until his death in 1908 at the age of eighty-seven. With this change, the department increased its pressure on the band. The Indian agent, George P. Cockburn, bypassed the new chief, Michel Dokis, Jr., and personally lobbied members of the band. Then he called a meeting on short notice with the sole object of getting the band to surrender the timber rights, liberally lacing the festivities with large quantities of illegal liquor. As a result of the vote, the Indian department sold the timber berths on June 17, 1908.

The chief's long struggle had, however, paid off in a commercial sense. The band did not receive the original pittance of $4 a head, nor the later promise of a one-time $131 a head. The timber sales produced more than a million dollars, and as a result every member of the band now receives fifty dollars a month.

These Indians are well off today because of the "stubborn waywardness of one old man" who loved the white pines of the Great Lakes, not for what they could produce in hard dollars but for themselves alone—for their soaring beauty, for the whisper of the breeze rustling through their needles, for their windblown silhouettes on the islands in the great bay, for the shade they offered on a steaming July afternoon, for the softness of the blanket they provided beneath the feet.

They are gone now, these evergreen sentinels, preserved only in the folk memories of the aboriginals, in the lusty Paul Bunyan stories and songs of another day, and in the canvases of a small group of painters who came up to Georgian Bay in the 1920s to record the few survivors of the Big Cut rising above the Precambrian rocks, lonely in their splendour, ragged in the wind that blows down the corridors of the lakes.

The government was clearly on the side of the timber interests. It used every tactic—threats, bribery, deception—to force Chief Dokis's band to sell its timber rights. An attempt was even made to change the Indian Act to force the "unreasonable" Indians to sell out.

The camboose shantymen

Forty-foot-long shanties, built without nails and chinked with moss, housed as many as fifty loggers in the days of the Big Cut. At the heart of each was the "camboose," an open hearth where fire burned day and night.

A typical camboose (from the French cambuse, *the provision room of a ship) is shown above. A twelve-foot square of logs with a foot-high earthen retaining wall, it stood in the middle of the shanty, burning continuously to provide the only heat, light, and cooking facility. In the early days there were neither utensils nor table. Everyone served himself and took what he needed from the pots bubbling over the fire. His own butcher knife also served as a fork. The camboose shanty originated in the Ottawa Valley and was adopted by Great Lakes loggers. At left, the neatly dressed female staff, who served Finnish lumber workers north of Sault Ste Marie, indicates more civilized conditions in the twentieth century.*

The logger's closest friend was his double-bitted axe, which had to be sharpened continually on the stone to retain the edge needed to penetrate the tough hide of the white pine.

By the turn of the century, Great Lakes lumber camps such as this one had achieved a luxury unknown in the days of the camboose. At left, in the cook shanty's dining room at Brillion, Wisconsin, a trio of violinists supplies a musical greeting. But in 1912 lumberjacks were still doing their laundry in the snow.

The abstract beauty
of the lake country

André Gallant travelled from the Thousand Islands to the far end of
Lake Superior to make these photographs. From the thunderous
majesty of Niagara Falls to Erie's dappled woods, from the abstract
patterns of Superior's pebbled beaches to a lonely mallard on
Georgian Bay, the lakes are captured here in all their splendour.

CHAPTER SEVEN

FIRE, STORM, AND HUMAN FRAILTY

ABOVE: **The Pelee Island lifeboat crew bends to the oars of their supposedly self-righting craft in the days of the great shipwrecks.** RIGHT: **Storm clouds gather over the lighthouse at the aptly named Thunder Bay.**

S A SMALL BOY I TRAVELLED MORE THAN ONCE ON A CRUISE SHIP DOWN THE COAST of Alaska and British Columbia from Skagway to Seattle. I cannot say I looked forward to the experience with anything but terror. Ships sank in those days, sometimes with all hands, ships such as the CPR's *Princess Sophia*, which had foundered on that very coast in 1918, bringing tragedy to almost every family in my hometown of Dawson. "The Wreck of the *Hesperus*" was a standard poem in our school reader, and so was the tale of the White Ship, which in 1120 took the life of an English prince. And, of course, there was the recent tragedy of the *Titanic*. I was certain that I and my fellow passengers would share their fate, and there was not a night during that voyage down the coast when I woke in my cabin without expecting the worst.

Our final destination was Ontario. How calm the waters of Lake Superior looked from the train after the angry Pacific! And when we reached my grandparents' home in Oakville, Lake Ontario seemed positively benign. We children sat on the rocky beach staring across the glassy expanse with no understanding of the power of the Great Lakes.

But in the early spring and especially in November that power can be awesome. I do not believe that many who live on these shores realize how potent it can be. The sailors know, of course. The lakes can be as menacing as the ocean itself, the waves as high as those that crash on foreign shores, the winds as terrible as the ones that wrecked the *Hesperus*. I was myself unaware of the chilling statistics until I dug into the history of these inland seas: since navigation opened on the Great Lakes, I learned, more than ten thousand vessels—*ten thousand!*—have been wrecked within these shores.

From Thunder Bay to the Thousand Islands, from Chicago to the Sault, their bones are strewn along lake bottoms and beaches for fifteen hundred miles. Hidden in the muck and silt and in the broken bowels of the lost ships themselves is a grisly ossuary—the skulls of thousands of sailors, long since polished clean by the abrasives of the deep. In a single decade—1863 to 1873—a total of 1,178 sailors went to their deaths

The lakes, which gave them their livelihood, became, in the end, their enemy. They went down with their vessels, the victims of founderings, collisions,

explosions, fire, and the killing storms that have savaged the Great Lakes since La Salle's little *Griffon* vanished into the mists more than three centuries ago.

A fortune in lost cargoes litters the lake bottoms waiting for new and more sophisticated salvage methods to raise them. This is especially true of Erie, which is conveniently shallow. A boatload of locomotives lies under the water near the mouth of the Detroit River. A small fortune of barrelled whiskey is hidden in the depths not far away. Oak and walnut timbers, as valuable as any metallic treasure, lurk in the shallows off Point Pelee.

The detritus of the immigrant ships that sank a century and more ago clutters the lake bottoms—beds and cradles, kitchen goods, casks of provisions, chests of clothing, farm implements, all brought to the promised land by Europe's teeming masses. Corn and wheat, pitch and sulphur, newsprint and salt—all lie hidden beneath the shattered decks and the storm-ravaged hatches of lost schooners.

It has been reckoned that at least eight hundred million dollars' worth of salvageable wrecks lies hidden beneath the surface of the Great Lakes—so many that in the latter half of the nineteenth century, one group of promoters actually proposed a scheme to drain Lake Michigan dry in order to aid salvage operations. That never happened, but more than one entrepreneur has cast a covetous eye at the real buried treasure beneath the waves. Divers have vainly tried to reach the sixty thousand dollars lost aboard the side-wheeler *Atlantic*, which went to the bottom of Lake Erie in 160 feet of water in 1852. One hundred thousand dollars' worth of gold ingots is believed to be secure in the safe of the *Westmoreland*, which sank in Lake Michigan in a storm. And there are those who believe that a mystery vessel that sank at Poverty Island near Escanaba has four and a half million in her safe.

Before the age of railways and automobiles, passenger vessels cruised the lakes, carrying first immigrants and later merrymakers. These always had auxiliary engines as well as sails, using side wheels at first, then propellers. Because the engines got in the way, it was difficult to carry bulk, and so the sailing schooner dominated the freight business until the late 1870s.

The day would come when the lake steamers would become floating palaces designed for the carriage trade, but in the 1830s, as the early immigration boom gathered speed in the United States, a Lake Erie ship was, in the words of one observer, "a floating Babel." He described the foredeck "appropriated to horses, mules, and oxen—wagons, carts, and coaches." The forecabin was "the resort of the vulgar and the vicious, the intemperate and the profane, with a gaping crowd of wonderers just out of the centre of confusion." Women and children were confined to the "prison-house" of the deck cabin, barred from the sitting room by the male passengers who discussed religion and politics over "the roaring of steam and fire, and the rattling of machinery ... and ... the trumpeted orders of the captain."

The hazard of fire was increased by the presence of the steam boilers, which had a habit of exploding. The firewood on deck might burst into flame from stray sparks. If fire occurred, the wooden ships, coated with inflammable varnish and paint, burned swiftly. There was no fire-fighting equipment.

The worst fires occurred on the lakes in the decade from 1840 to 1850. In that dreadful ten-year span one thousand souls lost their lives in floating fire-traps. Most were immigrants, like those on the side-wheeler *Erie*, which suffered the worst of all the fires on August 9, 1841. She had steamed out of Buffalo headed for Cleveland, Detroit, and Chicago when she suddenly erupted into flames. Incredibly, six painters had left their varnish and turpentine demi-johns on the boiler deck. One exploded, tearing a hole in the ship's side. A few

In November 1885, the CPR's new passenger liner, *Algoma*, the finest on the lakes, struck a reef off Greenstone Island near Isle Royale and broke in two. Fourteen survivors clung to the stern end for almost two days before being rescued.

minutes later the entire vessel was an inferno, whipped by a high wind. Of the two hundred passengers and crew aboard, one hundred and twenty were German-speaking Swiss immigrants.

A survivor was to describe the horrors that followed: "The air was filled with shrieks of agony and despair. The boldest turned pale. I shall never forget the wail of terror that went up from the poor German emigrants, who were huddled together on the forward deck. Wives clung to their husbands, mothers frantically pressed babes to their bosoms, and lovers clung madly to each other. . . . But if the scene forward was terrible, that aft was appalling, for there the flames were raging in their greatest fury. Some madly rushed into the fire; others, with a yell like a demon, maddened with the flames, which were all around them, sprang headlong into the waves."

Lifeboat after lifeboat was swamped by the rush to escape the flames. The ship's officers could not control the panic. The captain tried to reach the ladies' cabin where some hundred life preservers were stowed, but the fire beat him back. He ordered the steersman, Luther Fuller, to head for shore eight miles away. Fuller stayed at his post and burned to death. Of the two hundred passengers, only twenty-nine were saved, including a lone woman who seized a proffered oar and was hauled into a lifeboat.

Those early passenger vessels bore little resemblance to the splendid cruise ships that took holiday seekers out onto the breezy waters. Big Jim Hill, the man who helped get the Canadian Pacific under way in its early days and who later built the Great Northern Railway, had two luxury liners, *Northwest* and *Northland*, cruising the lakes in the early 1890s. As his brochures made clear, the staterooms were "finished in white mahogany and furnished with full-sized brass bedsteads in special designs. Rich rugs, beautiful lace spreads, tables, and, lastly, elegant private bathrooms, secure a luxurious comfort. The staterooms are lighted by 16-candle power lamps enclosed in ground glass globes . . . and extinguished by a switch placed adjacent to the berth."

In the heyday of lake travel the lake captains, in William Ratigan's words, were better known than celebrities today. "The captains of crack steamboats strutted into port, promenading the waterfront while admiring eyes took in their blue coats, brass buttons, nankeen trousers, white vests, low shoes, white stockings, ruffled shirts, high hats, jingling watch chains and seals. In the era of the Civil War they sported Prince Alberts and stovepipe lids and General Grant beards that gave them the appearance of Barnum's trained walruses."

And they went down with their ships when storm or fire struck. Indeed, there is one incredible instance of an entire crew of ten who refused to get into a coast guard lifeboat and insisted on going down with their captain aboard the ill-fated *Maplehurst*. There were, of course, exceptions to the old rule of the sea. When the popular lake steamer *G.P. Griffith* suffered an engine-room fire on June 17, 1870, the captain led the flight, throwing his wife, his two children, his mother, and himself overboard. He was never seen again.

By the 1870s, eighteen hundred sailing vessels—schooners, barques, brigantines, and sloops—were plying the lakes, loaded with grain, timber, coal, and oil: bulk cargoes that couldn't easily be loaded onto ships with cumbersome engines. Then in 1869 the shipbuilders designed a vessel, the *R.J. Hackett*, whose decks were clear because the machinery was located well aft. Thus was born the prototype of the modern lake freighter, with its long body and distinctive silhouette, an adaptation, really, of the mile-long trains of barges that had once carried timber to the mill towns of Michigan.

The exponents of sail responded to this threat by building bigger and better schooners. The biggest of all was the *David Dows*, launched in 1881, a 278-foot monster and the only five-master on the lakes. She carried seventy thousand yards of canvas, enough, as the Toledo *Blade* put it wickedly, "to furnish clean shirts to a large portion of the Democratic party in Ohio." But she was hard to handle and difficult to manoeuvre. She went out of control during a squall, rammed and sank another schooner, and was involved later in a second collision that killed four sailors. She ended her career ignominiously as a barge towed behind a tug until, on November 30, 1899, she foundered not far from Chicago. It might be said that the age of sail died with her.

The size of the new steam freighters was controlled only by the size of the locks in the Soo and Welland canals. By the nineties the new whalebacks were coming into use. They looked a bit like modern submarines, with flat bottoms, rounded tops, snout-like bows, and turrets instead of cabins. In one final burst of imagination, Alexander McDougall, the designer of the whaleback, created the only whaleback passenger craft ever built especially for the Columbian Exposition of 1893. His *Christopher Columbus* carried five thousand passengers at a time on her regular run from Chicago to the big fair. When she was scrapped in 1932 it was said that she had carried more passengers during her career than any vessel on the lakes.

By this time the long ships dominated the lakes. The first was the 605-foot *J. Pierpont Morgan*, launched in 1906. Her captain had commanded his first steamer two decades earlier. At that time it would have taken him two and a half

By the 1870s, eighteen hundred sailing vessels— schooners, barques, brigantines, and sloops— were plying the lakes, loaded with grain, timber, coal, and oil—bulk cargoes that couldn't easily be loaded onto ships with cumbersome engines.

years to carry as much ore as he could now carry in one single trip of the *Morgan* from Duluth to Cleveland. Today with the widening of the canals, lakers as long as three football fields move easily from one end of the lakes to the other—and much more safely.

But no ship is entirely safe, as the fates of the *Carl D. Bradley* in 1958 and the *Edmund Fitzgerald* in 1975 made clear. When the *Bradley* was launched in 1927 she was the longest ship on the lakes and was said to be unsinkable, the safest ship ever to ply the inland waters. But she broke in half as she tried to ride out a storm on Lake Michigan and plunged to the bottom. Of her thirty-four-man crew, only two survived.

Seventeen years later, the *Fitzgerald* met a similar fate, to be renowned in song and story. When launched in 1958 she too was the biggest ship on the lakes. She was equipped with enough lifeboats and life rafts (all of which could be launched in ten minutes) to carry the entire ship's company. She also carried twenty-four life buoys and eighty-three life preservers. There is no shred of evidence that any of her crew was able to make use of a single safety device. Her tragedy reminds us that there is no refuge from the storm.

She was travelling in the lee of Lake Superior's north shore within sight of the 767-foot ore carrier *Arthur M. Anderson,* both ships ignoring the shorter southern route, which was more exposed to gales. Gale warnings came at two that afternoon of November 10. Shortly after four, the *Fitzgerald*'s captain radioed to the *Anderson* that he had lost both his radars and was taking heavy seas over the deck in one of the worst storms he had ever experienced. The two ships kept in touch by radio telephone until 7:10 p.m. "How are you making out?" *Anderson*'s captain asked.

"We are holding our own," came the reply. That was the last message anyone ever had from the *Edmund Fitzgerald.*

Suddenly, she was gone. Her running lights vanished. Her radar blip disappeared from the screen. Her radio did not answer. The lake had swallowed her whole with her entire crew of twenty-nine. It happened so quickly that there was no hope for any of them.

How, in this modern age, could a 729-foot steel vessel vanish so suddenly? Had she foundered on a shoal, as some suggested? Had her cargo hold flooded, as others claimed? No one knows. She lies, broken in half, on the bottom of Lake Superior in Canadian waters, seventeen miles north-northwest of Whitefish Point, easily available to divers who, in 1995, brought up the ship's bell. But the manner of her death, like so many other lake tragedies, remains a mystery.

The Great Lakes hide the secrets to many maritime puzzles.

What of the *Bannockburn*, which left Port Arthur on the morning of November 21, 1902, with a load of grain for the lower lakes? The *Algonquin* spotted her that afternoon, a sturdy steel freighter with an unmistakable profile—three raked masts and a long, smoking tail funnel. That night the pilothouse crew of the *Huronic* saw her passing; in the years that followed more than one ship saw her, easily identifiable from her unique profile, slipping briefly out of the mists into the evening murk, a ghost ship like the famous *Flying Dutchman*. For the *Bannockburn* never reached port that bitter November. Fifteen months later a lifebelt bearing her name was washed ashore, and in 1928 an oar was found with *Bannockburn* carved on it—nothing else save brief appearances of an unidentified vessel with three raked masts and a tall tail funnel. The lakes are full of ghost ships, but the *Bannockburn* is easily the most famous.

Each of the lakes is a graveyard; each has its own hazards. Superior is so vast that its great rollers, some as high as a nine-storey building, resemble the limitless ocean itself. Huron's thirty thousand islands present thirty thousand hazards. Michigan is just the opposite, a three-hundred-mile corridor, unencumbered by island or headland, down which fierce gales can sweep without

A sailor in high boots clings to a safety rope lashed to the rail of an unidentified freighter as one of the storms of the 1940s washes over the decks.

hindrance, gathering force as they go. Erie is so shallow that no vessel can maintain a fixed course without running aground or colliding with another vessel. Only Ontario is relatively free of problems.

The inland seas are gigantic thermostats, storing up heat all summer. When fall comes, the vast polar air mass moves across the plains and slides into the bowl of the lakes. It sneaks under the warm-air layer that rises from the waters and forces that humid mass upward, causing hurricanes, snow, sleet, hail, and fog. The Great Lakes are the wildest of all the stormy regions of North America. When the masses of air collide, November becomes the wildest month of all.

Storms of the first magnitude occur at least once in every generation. The records go back to the big blow of November 1842 that littered the Canadian shore of Lake Erie with twenty broken vessels. In November 1869, another stem-winder of a storm raged for four days, leaving the wreckage of ninety-seven ships in its wake.

Some storms are named for the vessels they destroyed, such as the "*Alpena* storm" of October 1880, which wrecked ninety-four vessels and took 118 lives. The *Alpena*, which had steamed out of Grand Haven, Michigan, on a clear and balmy Friday evening, was never seen again nor were any of the eighty people aboard.

There are spring storms, too, when air masses collide over the lakes. In May 1894, a brutal spring gale "of almost mythic proportions" struck the American midwest and hovered for three days over the upper lakes. Milwaukee was badly hit. Two windjammers collided in the crowded harbour, killing six men in full view of throngs of onlookers. Chicago was far worse. Here, one hundred thousand spectators crowded to the beach front to watch the drama and the tragedy as ship after ship was driven down the lake and into the jammed harbour.

The schooner *Jack Thompson* had been running before the wind for the full length of the lake when it collided with the schooner *Rainbow* just beyond the government pier. The *Thompson* hit the beach broadside, her wreckage mingling with that of the *Rainbow*. Unable to manoeuvre, ship after ship was wrecked. The *Evening Star* hit the schooner *Myrtle*, veered off, limped for a distance along the beach, and then sank with all six hands. The *J. Loomis McLaren*'s tow post broke, sending gear flying and killing her mate. Hurled onto a beach one hundred yards away, she broke up as the crowd watched. The *C.G. Mixer* also lost her tug, drifted for miles, hit a sandbar, and was pounded to pieces by the storm that turned the heavy pieces of timber in her cargo into battering rams. Six other ships managed to struggle into port and survived.

The toll was appalling. The storm took twenty-seven lives and destroyed more than thirty-five schooners. It, too, helped hurry the death knell of sail: of the seventeen total losses, all were sailing vessels.

In the great storm of November 1905, thirty ships were wrecked on Lake Superior. The most awesome saga was that of the 430-foot steel freighter *Mataafa*, which tried to struggle back to port after an abortive foray into the storm-tossed waters. The angry lake thrust her against one of the harbour's piers and then swept her against the rocks, cracking her in two. As her stern settled into the water, the fires in her boilers were washed out. The temperature had dropped to minus 13°F, and for the nine men huddled in the aft cabin there was little hope. Forty thousand people kept a night-long vigil knowing they had come to watch nine men slowly freeze to death. The following morning when the winds died, rescue crews were able at last to make their way to the broken vessel. In the forward cabin the crewmen had huddled together for warmth and, by a miracle, were alive. But in the after cabin the rescuers found nine bodies, frozen solid. Some had to be chopped out of ice that had totally encased one man, the ship's engineer.

Several lake storms have been labelled "the worst," including that one, but the consensus is that the four-day storm that struck the inland seas early in November 1913 best merits that description. It totally destroyed nineteen ships, many with all hands, damaged fifty-two more, did millions of dollars in damage, and caused the deaths of 248 sailors. Frank Barcus, the chronicler of the storm, has called it "one of nature's giant pranks."

The buildup to the storm was predictable. Somewhere in the heart of the Great Lakes that cold November an atmospheric depression took form. On the night of Friday, November 7, a mass of polar air, born in the barren grounds of the Northwest Territories, was sucked toward the lakes, pouring into the low-pressure area like water tumbling over a cliff. The rotation of the earth caused this mass of frigid air, now mixed with snow, to change direction, moving south-west from the Sault to Michigan at ever-increasing speeds and carrying with it a thickening wall of snow. No lake captain could recall a storm of such unprece-dented violence. It raged without a break for sixteen hours, during which time the speed of the winds, always subject to rapid changes in direction, averaged sixty miles an hour. Nobody had seen such waves. They followed each other in quick succession, forty feet high. Often they ran counter to the direction of the wind, placing a terrible strain on the hull and engines of any vessel in their path.

"It is absolutely impossible to imagine the terror of those waves," one

The great storm of November 1913 totally destroyed nineteen ships, many with all hands, damaged fifty-two more, did millions of dollars in damage, and caused the deaths of 248 sailors.

The *Eastland* (ABOVE) suffered the worst disaster in the history of the lakes when she turned turtle at the dockside in Chicago in July 1915. The survivors, clinging to the vessel's upturned bottom (RIGHT), looked on in horror as lifeboats tried desperately to save some passengers. But 835 were drowned.

survivor, Captain James Watts of the steamer *J.F. Durston*, would recall. The rollers crashed over his bow with thunderous force and from both sides of the vessel, colliding in the centre of the deck, rushing wildly down toward the engine house, and breaking over it with the boom of a hundred cannons. Looking down from the pilothouse into the trough between the waves, Watts said, "was like looking far down into a seething valley during an upheaval of nature." Watts survived after enduring a seventy-two-hour watch without a wink of sleep.

He was one of the fortunate ones. Two big freighters, the *Hydrus* and the *James Carruthers*, taking advantage of a lull in the storm, steamed out of the Soo locks, only to find the storm closing in again. A floating navigational beacon had been blown two miles off its course. Neither freighter, groping blindly in the gloom, was ever seen again.

The lake cities were equally savaged. At Milwaukee the waves hammered a new breakwater into fragments. Chicago lost a park project that had taken eight years to complete. Parts of Michigan and Ontario were blacked out; it took forty-eight hours before telegraph and telephone communications were restored.

Cleveland, paralysed by a twenty-one-inch snowfall, was isolated. The lights went out, the telephone and telegraph stopped working. The streetcars were stalled by eight-foot drifts and their passengers marooned. Union Station was jammed with travellers who couldn't travel, and the railroad tracks were blocked by fallen poles and tangles of wires. It took twelve hours for a single train to struggle through the centre of town.

Cleveland's people had no real conception of the toll the storm had taken. Only later did they begin to comprehend the dimensions of the tragedy. Twenty freighters owned by Cleveland businessmen had been totally destroyed. Worse, 186 Cleveland seamen had been lost with their ships.

The first news of a wrecked vessel did not reach the city until the Monday after the storm had subsided. Then reports came in of a ship apparently without a hull, masts, or smokestack, floating in Lake Huron. The veteran salvage captain Tom Reid went out in his tug and came face-to-face with a bizarre spectacle, the strangest he'd ever seen. A big steel freighter, coated with ice, was floating bottom up, its bow thirty feet out of the water, its stern submerged. It could not be identified because its name was hidden beneath the waves. What was this "mystery" ship, as the press called it? Only divers probing around the submerged stern could tell, but the weather was too rough for an undersea search.

Meanwhile, bodies from various wrecks were being washed ashore, many wearing lifebelts that bore the name of their ship. This was the only way in which rescuers could identify vessels that seemed to have vanished into thin air. But there was another puzzle. How was it that some of the bodies of sailors identified as having been members of the crew of the *Charles S. Price* were washed ashore wearing lifebelts from the *Regina*? The two ships had not been travelling together; indeed, when last seen they were fifteen miles apart. What had happened?

The 524-foot *Price* was a new freighter, scarcely three years old, considered able to withstand any storm and equipped with every available safety device. Now she had vanished from the lake. A week passed without any clue to her fate. It must have been swift, for the body of her steward, Herbert Jones, was found still wearing the apron he used when about to prepare a meal. It was frozen to his corpse.

Six more days went by. When the storm finally died, a diver went down to try to identify the mystery vessel. And there on the submerged stern, in big black letters, was her name: *Charles S. Price*. A few days later as the air trapped in her hull bubbled to the surface, she went to the bottom with two questions still unanswered: How could this big, flat-bottomed ore carrier, stabilized by a full load of coal, possibly have turned turtle? The waves must have been truly mountainous on that tragic weekend. And why were some of her crew wearing the *Regina*'s life preservers?

In 1986, a diver finally located the wreck of the *Regina* some fifteen miles from the last resting place of the *Price*. All the evidence suggested she had sunk swiftly with little warning. Apparently she had been at anchor when the storm hit. How did some of the *Price*'s crewmen get her lifebelts? No one to this day has been able to account for one of the enduring mysteries of the Great Lakes.

Yet the greatest of all disasters in the history of the inland seas wasn't caused by a storm. The *Eastland*, one of the most popular excursion boats ever to sail Lake Michigan, didn't founder far out in the open water. She met her end at the Clark Street Bridge dock in Chicago on July 24, 1915, drowning 835 people, the majority between the ages of fifteen and thirty. The *Eastland* had such a perfect safety record that her owners had offered a five-thousand-dollar reward to anyone who could prove that she was not seaworthy. She was known as the Speed Queen of the Lakes because of the powerful twin propellers that drove her through the water at twenty-two miles an hour.

On this day she was overloaded. By 7:20 that July morning—a Saturday—

she was jammed with twenty-five hundred passengers who piled on board to the music of a steam calliope, all eager for a holiday cruise on the lake. In order to raise the boat to the level of the gangway, her crew had pumped eight hundred tons of water out of her ballast tanks so that gangplanks could be placed between the ship and the dock.

As the passengers came aboard they crowded along the side of the upper decks nearest the dock to listen to the music and to watch the families come aboard. That caused the ship to list slightly toward the dock. To straighten her out, the crew pumped four hundred tons of water into the tanks on the far side of the ship. On the dock side the ballast tanks were now empty. Had it not been for the lines holding her in position, *Eastland* would have listed badly toward the lake.

The captain had been ashore on ship's business. When he arrived on deck and ordered the mooring lines cast off, he knew nothing of the water ballast. At this point the *Eastland* was listing *away* from the dock. At that moment a fireboat moved up the river, and the passengers crowded to the outer rail to watch it pass. Only then did one of them notice that the folding deck chairs were sliding down the deck from starboard to port. Suddenly the refreshment stand tore loose. A woman screamed just as the listing ship lost her balance and turned turtle, hurling hundreds of passengers into the river and trapping hundreds more in cabins below deck.

Eyewitness accounts of the disaster are heart rending:

. . . We could see the people in the water. Men were holding women by the hair. The screaming was awful. People were calling out looking for loved ones. . . .

. . . others in the water panicked . . . I saw many a drowning person push someone else under in his struggle to stay above the water. Mothers and fathers ranged the shore, screaming the names of their children. The bodies of the dead floated past, ignored by the rescuers who were trying their best to save the living. . . .

The *Eastland* disaster was a freak, but a freak that might have been avoided. It raised many questions about the Inspection Service of the American government. The investigation that followed urged changes in the laws regarding the loading of boats, making local inspectors more accountable to their superiors. If those laws had been in effect in 1915, the *Eastland* disaster need not have happened. The ship herself was salvaged and restored to duty, but not as a passenger liner. She ended her days as the USS *Wilmette*, one of the finest Naval Reserve training ships in the United States.

The great storms still ravage the lakes. In November 1940, "the war of

Suddenly the refreshment stand tore loose. A woman screamed just as the listing ship lost her balance and turned turtle, hurling hundreds of passengers into the river and trapping hundreds more in cabins below deck.

The luxury liner *Noronic* was destroyed by fire while moored at a Toronto dock on September 6, 1949. Most passengers were asleep in their beds; some were ashore; 118 died.

weather fronts" attacked the lakes with a fury similar to the great blow of 1913. Described as one of the worst on record for "magnitude, intensity, and diversity," with winds reaching one hundred miles an hour, it did not leave in its wake the carnage attributed to the earlier hurricane. Though two big freighters went down with all hands—a total of fifty-seven deaths—the losses were not on a par with those of 1913. The day of wooden ships was over. Modern weather forecasting, channel and navigational aids, ship-to-shore telephones, and steel hulls had made the difference. No more than three vessels are now lost annually.

The *Noronic*, operated by Canada Steamship Lines, docked at Toronto at 6:00 p.m. on Friday, September 6, 1949. She had just completed the first leg of a luxury cruise that was to take her passengers from Detroit and Cleveland to the Thousand Islands of the St. Lawrence. A handsome, four-decked floating palace, she sported picture windows, writing and music rooms, an observation saloon, a buffet bar, even a beauty parlour. Since she would be docked in Toronto for twenty-four hours, many of her 695 passengers and crew went ashore to shop or sightsee. Most were back on board and asleep when, at a quarter past one in the morning, a passenger noticed a wisp of smoke creeping from under the door of the linen cupboard. At that time the ship was in the hands of a skeleton crew of fifteen. The passenger managed to find a bellboy, and the two tried to stifle the fire. It was remarked later that they might just as well have tried "to put out hell with their fountain pens." In a few moments the passageway was in flames and the ship an inferno.

Eighteen fire engines and two fireboats rushed to the scene and spent five hours trying to douse the flames. As far as could be determined, 118 passengers died, smothered in their sleep by the smoke, some trapped in their cabins, some locked in each other's arms. Tallying of the dead and missing was complicated by the fact that some of the male passengers had taken advantage of the cruise to forsake hearth and home and spirit girlfriends or mistresses away on a brief holiday.

An investigation found a lack of planning for the eventuality of a fire and also a failure of the crew to take action to wake the passengers and guide them to safety. Both the American and the Canadian governments moved to enforce better safety regulations on lake passenger vessels, but no ship in service could afford to meet those new procedures. Nor, with the passenger traffic on the lakes declining, did anyone want to build new ones. The luxury cruise ships were gone from the lakes along with the schooners and the barques and the early freighters. The thousand-foot bulk carriers monopolize the inland seas today, their long, low profiles contrasting with the bright little sailboats of the merrymakers.

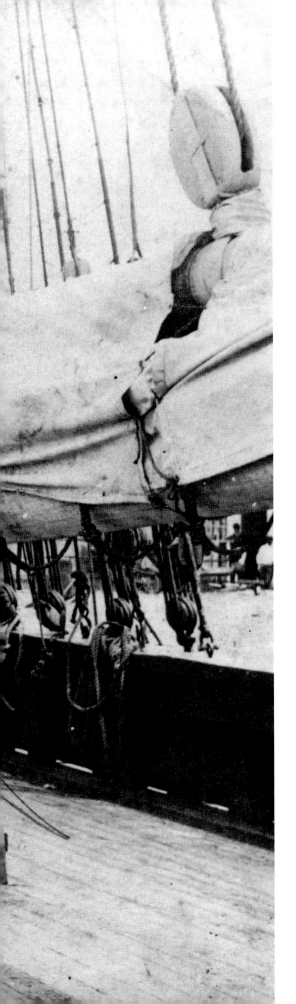

The working lakes

The inland seas together form a gigantic industrial complex, as important as General Motors, employing thousands of workers—fishermen, dredgers, crane operators, canal workers, and, of course, the sailors who man the ships.

In the 1870s the schooner was the queen of the lakes. As the photograph on the far left makes clear, her crew did not wear the typical sailor's blue but dressed in their own style in every type of cap, hat, waistcoat, and jacket.

TOP: *The Collingwood fishing fleet in harbour in the 1880s. Most of the boats shown here were built by the Watts family—double-ended clinker-built craft that were speedy and handled well in Georgian Bay's shallow waters. One in three residents earned an income directly from the Collingwood shipyard.*
BOTTOM: *Ojibwa fishermen pole their boats through the turbulent rapids of the St. Mary's River at the turn of the century.*
OPPOSITE: *One of the last of the great cruise ships, the SS* North American, *pulls into her dock at Chicago in 1954 loaded with holidayers who have just spent a week on the water.*

GEORGIAN BAY LINE

Great Lakes Cruises

FOR INFORMATION
SEE YOUR
TRAVEL AGENT

S.S. NORTH AMERICAN
SAILS FROM THIS DOCK EVERY SAT 4 PM

S.S. NORTH AMERICA

FROM THIS DOCK EVERY SAT. 4 PM
2200 MILES · 7 DAYS

Always America First
CHICAGO TRIBUNE

TOP: *Dredging a channel at the Algoma Steel Company's iron ore dock,*
Sault Ste Marie, July 8, 1914.
BOTTOM: *Workmen take a breather at the coal docks in Duluth Harbor in*
the summer of 1900.

Wheat is drawn into an Erie Canal grain elevator by an endless bucket line. A shovel rigged on ropes scoops the grain into an area where it can be reached.

It is more than a thousand miles, as the gull flies, from Duluth at the far western tip of Lake Superior to the Thousand Islands of the St. Lawrence. For most of that distance the sailor rarely sees the shore. The freighters carry everything from oil, grain, and ore to cargoes of automobiles, like this load of 1937 Chryslers (RIGHT) parked at the Milwaukee docks.

CHAPTER EIGHT

SAGAS OF THE BIG DITCHES

M ARIE-JOSEPH-PAUL-YVES-ROCH-GILBERT DU MOTIER, MARQUIS DE LAFAYETTE, "the hero of two worlds," was in a jubilant mood when he arrived at Lockport on Bastille Day, 1825, and embarked on a special barge awaiting him on the partly finished Erie Canal.

Why shouldn't he be jubilant? The president of the United States had himself supplied the barge. In spite of Lafayette's revolutionary zeal, his halo had been tarnished in his homeland because of his monarchist sympathies. But in the United States he was received with a wild adulation that tickled his considerable vanity. Now, with his triumphal tour of the nation reaching its climax, his hosts were eager to show off the greatest engineering work of its day—"that grand canal, which in tightening the bonds of the American union, spreads comfort and abundance in the wilds through which it passes."

The Grand Canal! That is how the Americans saw it: a touch of the Renaissance here in the backwoods of Upper New York. Even as Lafayette boarded the barge, one thousand workmen were still blasting a strait through a seven-mile Appalachian ridge, two miles of which were solid rock. The cut was almost four storeys deep. A very grand canal indeed.

The Erie Canal would transform the Great Lakes. It would populate the south shore of Lake Erie, creating new cities—Buffalo, Cleveland, and Toledo—out of the wilderness of upstate New York and Ohio. It would provide an alternative and cheaper route from the lakes to New York City, and it would launch a new era of canal travel that Canada would be forced to emulate. The Erie Canal was the catalyst that led eventually to the linking of all the lakes with the St. Lawrence River to produce the greatest inland traffic system in history.

All along the canal new communities were springing up. At Rochester, Lafayette's barge was met by a flotilla of decorated boats and crowds of spectators waving flags. A ceremonial stage had been erected atop the aqueduct that carried the canal over the river—another wonder of the age. At Rome, Utica, and Schenectady, throngs of children leaned over bridges and showered him with flowers. It was not just Lafayette they were cheering, it was the Grand Canal itself.

More than three hundred and fifty miles in length and six years in the building, it had cost New York State a hefty seven million dollars. But now Buffalo and all of western New York would be tied to the Atlantic by way of the Mohawk gap in the Appalachian chain and the Hudson River. As one speaker at the sod-turning ceremony at Rome, N.Y., declared, "By this great highway, unborn millions will easily transport their surplus production . . . and hold a useful and profitable intercourse with all the maritime nations of the earth."

It was truly a remarkable engineering feat. At that time there were no bulldozers, no steam shovels, no earth-moving machinery. The Irish labourers were paid forty-seven cents for a fourteen-hour day. At first they used spades and wheelbarrows in the European style but soon switched—on dry ground, at least—to ploughs and scrapers. There was no adequate engineering training available. The canal itself became a school.

To surmount the five-hundred-foot rise in elevation up to and over the rock ridge at Lockport—the same escarpment that created Niagara Falls—eighty-two locks would be needed. No supply roads existed. Horses and men would do all the work. Rivers and streams were crossed with aqueducts. Rock was blasted away with black powder; dynamite had not yet been invented.

The plan for an interior canal, giving the United States its own outlet from the Great Lakes, had been bruited about since the century's turn. The War of 1812 halted all efforts to dig the big ditch. From the American point of view, the only outlet from the four internationally owned lakes ran through a foreign power.

The burgeoning communities in western New York State were clamouring for a cheaper water route. With the help of a new governor, De Witt Clinton, they got one. Small wonder that church bells rang and crowds cheered when the middle section of the canal—ninety-four miles—was opened on the Fourth of July, 1820, a mere three years after the project was started. It produced, in the words of the Rochester *Telegraph*, "emotions which those only who felt them can conceive."

Not everyone was so ebullient. The Tammany Hall machine that controlled New York City politics was violently opposed to this "monument of weakness." Nevertheless, two years before the canal was finished, one Michigan newspaper was able to report that "the spirit of canalling is the rage of the day." The Canal Era had begun.

The Grand Canal was formally opened on October 16, 1825, a little more than three months after Lafayette's triumphal arrival. In the statewide celebration that marked the event, some of the guns used by Perry on Lake Erie twelve years before were fired to greet the *Seneca Chief* from Buffalo. She carried two kegs of Lake Erie water, logs of native cedar from Erie, products of the American lake states, and an entire Indian canoe, crafted on Superior's shore. Jess Hawley, a Rochester politician, hailed the canal as "the greatest public utility . . . in the world." It had been a state-owned project from the start.

A flotilla of canal barges followed the horse-drawn *Seneca Chief*, applauded by thousands who jammed the banks. Every village along the route was festooned with floral arches and banners. Cannon fired; bands played; fireworks exploded. At ten on the morning of November 2, the flotilla reached Albany to a twenty-one-gun salute. After the usual parade and banquet the procession proceeded down the Hudson. Two days later it reached New York City's East River for a Grand Aquatic Display involving forty-six steamers, pilot boats, barges, and naval craft.

With the steamers towing the smaller craft, the flotilla moved out to Sandy Hook, and there, from a U.S. naval schooner, one of the kegs of Erie water was slowly poured into the Atlantic. Vials from the Ganges, the Nile, the Rhine, and twelve other great rivers of the world were united with the salt ocean. In the celebrations that followed, a replica of a canal boat made entirely of maple sugar went into a special box crafted by Duncan Phyfe as a gift for Lafayette, who had returned to France.

A spirit of international co-operation marked the event. British bands played "Yankee Doodle." Americans responded with the strains of "God Save the King." Yet no hands-across-the-border amity could disguise the fact that a great deal of lucrative Great Lakes traffic would no longer go to Montreal, being diverted to American ports at considerable saving. Goods that had been shipped from Buffalo to Montreal at a cost of thirty dollars a ton could now be transported to New York City for fifteen.

None of that hard truth was lost on William Hamilton Merritt, himself no Yankee lover. Merritt came of United Empire Loyalist stock, and he himself had been in the forefront of the fighting in the recent war. As leader of a volunteer group of Provincial Dragoons, he was, by the age of twenty, a seasoned guerrilla fighter, veteran of a dozen skirmishes, hair-breadth escapes, shoot-outs, midnight rides, sleepless nights, sudden forays, and hurried retreats. When tactics demanded it, he had risked an American firing squad by donning an enemy uniform and affecting a Yankee twang to confuse the enemy. Captured at the Battle of Lundy's Lane, he sat out the rest of the war as a prisoner. But by then he knew every wrinkle of the Niagara Peninsula from Newark to Welland.

No hands-across-the-border amity could disguise the fact that a great deal of lucrative Great Lakes traffic would no longer go to Montreal but be diverted to American ports at considerable saving.

149

That battle had been fought in the dark with the roar of the great cataract echoing that of the cannon. Quite clearly a canal was needed to circumvent that formidable obstacle and link Lakes Ontario and Erie. If Canadians didn't build it, Merritt was sure his former enemies would—and on their own side of the border. That would never do.

Even as Merritt was acquiring land and building his milling and distillery business at St. Catharines and Twelve Mile Creek, the Americans were forging ahead with the Erie Canal. But before the job was done Merritt and his supporters had obtained a charter to build a private canal by way of Chippawa and Twelve Mile Creek. Thus did the former guerrilla fighter mix nationalism with sound business. Montreal's commercial supremacy was threatened. Business interests in both Upper and Lower Canada had good reason to be concerned about the possibility of that city's decline. The Americans had tried to invade Canada several times during the war. What if they tried again? A decade after the war's end they were still the enemy in Canadian eyes.

Merritt was certain he could get further financial support in Great Britain in addition to that supplied by the provincial legislature. From its "peculiar and most favourable situation" the proposed canal would quickly pay for itself and "a general tide of prosperity will be witnessed on the whole line and surrounding country." He needed the British press on his side, but the snooty editor of the *Times* didn't want to see this upstart colonial. Merritt persisted and was finally permitted five minutes—no more. That was all he needed.

He unrolled a map on the editor's desk and prepared to give him a geography lesson: "Here is Lake Erie. Here is the Falls of Niagara. This is Lake Ontario. This is the St. Lawrence and the Atlantic. And here is the route of the great Welland Canal." The editor needed no more convincing, and the *Times* played an important part in helping Merritt raise funds overseas. At the head of the list of stockholders was the name of the prime minister himself, the Duke of Wellington, who took fifty shares.

The conditions under which these canal builders—largely immigrant Irishmen—worked were as appalling as those endured by the Erie Canal labourers. The first Welland Canal was dug virtually by hand by men using picks and shovels, wheelbarrows, scrapers, and carts drawn by horses or mules. Even these primitive implements were hard to come by. Great Britain did not export spades and shovels to Canada; these had to be brought in from the United States, at high import duties. Many of the contractors were Americans who had learned their trade on the Erie—men such at Oliver Phelps, who devised a primitive earth-moving machine. Again, the canal builders had to work out their own technique on the job to chop up the matted turf or to cut and remove roots and stumps. Often enough the only solution was simply brute force.

The Irish muckers worked in a gruel of water and mud. "They waded knee deep in black muck, wheeled, dug, hewed, bore heavy burdens on their shoulders, exposed at all times to every change of temperature, till stricken down with fever, they took refuge in the shanties, and in the narrow bunks trembled with disease." Because water from the marshes was polluted, they drank dippersful of whiskey passed around regularly by "water boys." It was filthy, back-breaking toil, paid for by a pittance and overseen by hard-driving contractors. Men often worked like mules, carrying slings on their shoulders attached to sacks of mud that had to be removed by hand from the excavation site. Rock was blasted by gunpowder stuffed into hand-drilled holes—the fragments to be carried away again on the backs of men.

The canal was completed in 1829, but by the 1840s, after it was taken over

The route of the Welland Canal sometimes creates the illusion that huge lake freighters are ploughing through a forest of deciduous trees.

by the government, it could no longer handle the new, bigger ships. Its wooden locks and iron hardware had fallen into disrepair, and a new version with stone locks was needed to accommodate these vessels, including passenger steamers. A third-generation canal, opened in 1887, was built to remove all through shipping from the thriving downtown centres of Thorold and St. Catharines. The canal had created its own problems: it brought so much business along its route that it had to be re-excavated and moved. At a greater depth of fourteen feet, this new, shorter route allowed larger vessels to pass into Lake Erie. The Americans' Grand Canal was no longer a threat.

The canal quite literally created new communities and caused the decline of older ones. Because of its location, St. Catharines became the key industrial town on the Niagara Peninsula. It was the heavy traffic that caused the canal to be routed outside the downtown area, and more bridges had to be built to span it. The fourth canal, visualized in 1911 but not completed until 1932, was twice as deep as the third and operated with only eight locks instead of twenty-six. But again, the traffic problems created by the burgeoning towns along its route forced another change. Welland, one of the creations of the canal, was no longer a village. Originally the waterway had coiled through its business section. But by 1965 a bypass was needed to circumvent the town. Eight years later it was finished.

The opening of Merritt's original Welland Canal linked the lower lakes together in a single transportation corridor. By 1848, with new canals built to circumvent the rapids along the upper St. Lawrence, an uninterrupted water highway, albeit only nine feet in depth, ran from Montreal to Sault Ste Marie.

The Sault rapids continued to be the problem. They isolated the greatest of all the lakes from the other four. Superior lies some twenty feet higher than Huron, with most of the drop occurring in a single turbulent mile of the St. Mary's River. No craft, be it barquentine, sloop, or even canoe, could negotiate that fierce barrier, as the North West Company had realized years before. The company had built a canal of sorts—not much more than a ditch with two primitive locks. It was forgotten for seventy years and rediscovered only in 1889.

Long before that it was obvious that a proper canal was needed at the Sault. By the 1840s the copper rush in Michigan had reached fever pitch. But the ingots on the Keweenaw Peninsula could not be shipped by water to the lower lakes because the Sault blocked all passage. Any increase of traffic that might be fostered on the lakes could only benefit the Welland Canal, now the property of the Canadian government. Already three-quarters of its business came from ships travelling between American ports. The Niagara *Chronicle* urged Ottawa to wake up. "The Americans are not asleep about a ship canal round the Sault, and our Government should look out or they will be superseded to the great object which has been repeatedly urged upon them."

But colonial Canada slumbered. In 1852, Samuel Keefer, the chief engineer of the Department of Public Works, made specific suggestions for a ten-foot-deep ship canal at the Sault. Nothing came of it, but that same year the Americans acted. The U.S. government set aside three-quarters of a million acres for a canal, and within a year sixteen hundred men were at work on the project. A devastating cholera epidemic killed one in ten, but in spite of that the canal was complete by midsummer, 1855. At last the five Great Lakes were linked together. Now the riches of Superior could be tapped.

Canada paid dearly for her neglect of a canal route around the rapids of the St. Mary's. In 1870, Louis Riel and his Métis followers were in open revolt on the Manitoba prairie. Out across the Shield came Colonel Garnet Wolseley—who would be the prototype for W.S. Gilbert's "model of a modern major general" in *The Pirates of Penzance*—with three hundred and fifty British regulars and several hundred volunteers. But when they tried to ship their supplies and arms through the Soo Canal aboard the steamer *Chicora*, the ship was stopped by the Americans, possibly because she had been a blockade-runner during the Civil War. An international furore followed, and the ship was finally granted passage; but Canada smarted under the public knowledge that a foreign power controlled communication with the West.

In spite of the clamour for an all-Canadian water route, the Canadian government moved with colonial languor. By the time it was ready to proceed—1888—the Americans had built two Soo Canals and were completing a third along "the busiest one mile in the world." When the Canadian canal was finally completed in 1894, its single lock was the largest in North America. To match similar improvements on the other side, its depth was increased to twenty-two feet, giving it a four-foot advantage over the Americans. That did not last long. The U.S. army engineers continued to widen, deepen, and improve their own canal. The bulk traffic avoided Canada. By 1914, the largest vessels on the lakes, 625 feet long, could be locked through two at a time on the American side. By 1919 the Americans had a four-foot advantage in depth. American traffic doubled, Canadian traffic declined almost fourfold. While the Americans expanded their facilities to deal with the big new vessels, the Canadians continued to service ships that belonged to a previous century.

In spite of the clamour for an all-Canadian water route, the Canadian government moved with colonial languor. By the time it was ready to proceed, the Americans had built two Soo Canals and were completing a third.

A superfreighter in one of the Welland Canal locks—a familiar sight for any tourist motoring from Toronto to Niagara Falls. The vessels became so large that the canal was rebuilt three times to accommodate them and the growing traffic caused by the new communities that sprang up along the route.

Nonetheless, for all of the 1920s, the Canadian Soo Canal dominated the passenger trade. While the Americans concentrated on bulk cargoes of ore and wheat, the Canadians promoted what the Sault *Star* called "one of Canada's most wonderful waterways, the wildly beautiful scenery on the shores of Lake Superior."

When the next war came in 1939, the Soo Canals were called "the jugular vein of the Allied war effort." Few realized that this strategically placed strip of water was the most heavily defended spot on the continent. Steel was the key to victory, and the main source of domestic iron lay in the Mesabi. If long-range bombers destroyed this link between the two upper lakes, the resultant iron famine could cripple the Allies.

The decline of the passenger trade in the last half of the century made the Canadian canal effectively obsolete. In 1988, after a crack developed in the big lock, it went out of service, leaving all the business to the Americans, whose new Poe lock, built in 1968, was the first to accommodate the thousand-foot freighters.

Meanwhile, pressure for a deeper passage piercing the heart of the continent and carrying oceangoing vessels to the iron deposits and grain elevators of Superior had grown steadily. Immediately after Confederation, the Canadian government had deepened the existing canals around the rapids of the St. Lawrence to fourteen feet. It soon became apparent that this wasn't enough. Passage through the twenty-two locks on the big river was maddeningly slow. As ships grew bigger, more and more found they couldn't get through at all.

But the idea of a deep waterway from the Gulf of St. Lawrence to Thunder Bay and Duluth met with such bitter opposition that its construction was delayed for half a century. In the 1920s, Canadians themselves were cool. The idea of going into a junior partnership with a powerful and unpredictable foreign nation rankled. By 1932, however, with the fourth Welland Canal complete and the Erie Canal deepened to twelve feet, Canada signed an agreement to share equally the costs of an international waterway, twenty-seven feet deep. That treaty was effectively shelved by the U.S. Senate until 1954.

The American anti-Seaway lobby had its birth in 1895 when the first proposals were made to Congress. Some years later the lobby was formally organized under the innocuous title of National St. Lawrence Project. It numbered 250 organizations as members and was, in the words of the muckraking journalist George Seldes, "one of the greatest combinations of money and power in the history of America." The Seaway opponents included the Morgan, Mellon, and Duke interests, the Aluminum Company of America, General Electric Corporation, and the powerful railroad lobby.

These forces used a variety of techniques, such as referring to it as an "Iceway," even going so far as to co-opt midwestern isolationists by predicting that it would allow British warships to enter the Great Lakes. The lobby sent a blizzard of slanted editorials and news reviews to fourteen thousand newspapers that used them without revealing their source. In one instance, six hundred papers published identical items without attribution.

Proponents of the Seaway couldn't match the lobby in wealth or influence. They had to wait for a change in attitude that finally came in the late forties with the discovery of iron in Labrador. That, with the decline of high-grade ore in the Mesabi, gave impetus to any proposal to ship ore cheaply out of Sept-Îles to the steel mills of Cleveland and Pittsburgh. At the same time the Canadian commitment was stiffening. By 1951, Canada made it clear that she was prepared to build the Seaway alone. It was no longer a question of whether the Seaway would be built; as Harry Truman said, the question was whether the United States would participate.

At last "one of the most incredible engineering and construction jobs ever attempted" was given the go-ahead. On the St. Lawrence the old canals and locks were torn apart and replaced by seventy miles of new channel. Engineers dammed the historic Long Sault rapids to form Lake St. Lawrence, drowning 225 farms, 8 villages, 35 miles of highway, the homes of 6,500 people, and the site of the historic battle of Crysler's Farm in 1813. The great dam, one hundred and fifty feet high, deepened the new waterway from fourteen feet to twenty-seven and generated more than a billion watts of electricity.

At first, the Seaway thrived. Business reached its peak in 1977. Then it began a long decline. Only recently has there been a slight upturn, thanks to the booming steel market in the United States, which is fed by coal and iron brought to the mills by lake traffic. The decline of the traditional grain markets is one reason why the Seaway ceased to show a profit; much of that trade now goes through Vancouver.

The Seaway finds itself in a bind similar to those faced by earlier canals. Oceangoing ships have grown so large that the waterway can't handle them. But how can it rebuild when its present lock fees are so great that many carriers are lobbying for a reduction? It costs about fifty thousand dollars to lock just one vessel through from the Lake Erie end of the Welland to Montreal. When the Seaway opened, its proponents predicted that business would thrive along the route. But on the Seaway, as the Authority's president, Glendon Stewart, has said, "there are too many ships and too many ports chasing too little cargo." Thus, as in the past, the newest canal system on the Great Lakes finds itself a victim of its own success.

But there is a another problem, one that no one, neither proponent nor opponent of a waterway for ocean vessels, foresaw. I can remember how everybody in Canada wanted the Seaway and how we despised the railways and the power companies for their greed in opposing it for selfish commercial reasons. Perhaps had they been able to divine what the Seaway would bring they might have swayed some of us. But, of course, no one realized that the new canals at Welland and the Sault would open up the entire Great Lakes system to foreign predators or that the presence of oceangoing ships on these inland waters would bring intruders from as far away as the Caspian Sea.

Since the 1800s at least 140 aquatic invaders have entered the Great Lakes.

What, for example, was a river ruffe doing in Duluth harbour on Lake Superior back in 1986? This ruffe is a Eurasian species from the Caspian Sea, a nuisance fish capable of explosive population growth. It arrived in the ballast water of an oceangoing freighter—but only after the St. Lawrence Seaway was in operation.

The Seaway has a lot to answer for. Almost half of all invasions took place after it opened. Since ocean freighters began dumping their ballast, the lakes have teemed with exotic species ranging from the spiny water flea to the zebra mussel. Yet even before the Seaway, fish stocks were devastated by species brought to the lakes through earlier canals.

The sea lamprey was one of these—an eel-like fish that kills its victims by attaching itself to their bodies and sucking them dry of blood and flesh. The lamprey was confined to Lake Ontario until the fourth Welland Canal was opened in 1932, allowing it to follow an upstream course into Lake Erie. The result was overwhelming. By 1937 the lamprey had moved into both Lakes Huron and Michigan and almost half of Lake Superior. In less than twenty years the lake trout fisheries in both Huron and Michigan were wiped out. The parasites even attacked trout caught in nets so that the only harvest was nets full of dead fish.

This extraordinary devastation led to what has been called "one of the largest and most intensive efforts to control a vertebrate predator ever attempted." The key has been a highly selective chemical lampricide called TFM. By spraying the lamprey's spawning beds, scientists have held the predator's population in check since the 1960s.

The alewife, a small, silvery, shad-like member of the herring family, entered Lake Erie in 1932 by way of the Welland Canal and Superior through the Soo Canal by 1954. This skinny little fish doesn't eat other fish; it causes them to die out because it gobbles up the zooplankton on which so many species—lake herring, smelt, perch—also feed. Since the first alewife was found in Lake Michigan in 1949, the population has exploded. Fifteen years later, 90 percent of all the fish in that lake—by *weight*—were alewives.

There is one positive, if ironic, side to the alewife invasion. For the sake of sport fishermen, the lakes are being stocked with salmon and trout to replace the native species that have vanished. Their primary food source, it turns out, is alewives.

There are worse problems. The most devastating of the invaders, again from the Caspian Sea, is a thumb-sized, brown-and-white-striped clam-like creature that can glue itself to any hard surface—buoys, piers, pipes, hulls,

The Seaway has a lot to answer for. Almost half of all foreign predators appeared after it opened. Since ocean freighters began dumping their ballast, the lakes have teemed with exotic species, ranging from the spiny water flea to the zebra mussel.

The steel works at Hamilton Harbour on the route of the St. Lawrence Seaway. In spite of optimistic prophecies, the great waterway has failed to live up to its promise. Ocean ships have grown so large it can no longer handle them.

rocks. When two zoology students found one of these zebra mussels in Lake St. Clair in 1988, the pests were already well established. By 1989 they had crossed Lake Huron and by 1990 were infesting all five Great Lakes.

Prolific is hardly the word for these "animal weeds," as they've been called. I have walked along the beaches of Pelee Island crunching through a depth of shells that reaches almost to the ankle. A female can lay a million eggs in a year. In certain parts of Erie, their population has reached more than six hundred thousand a square yard. They cling to everything, including each other, building huge colonies several layers thick that clog all manner of pipes and outlets.

In December 1989, millions of zebra mussels jammed the intake of the water treatment plant at Monroe, Michigan, and shut down the town for two days. Industries, schools, restaurants, bars—all had to close. The neighbouring power plant was also under siege. In the words of one official, it had "turned into a zebra mussel nursery." This has become a costly business. Detroit Edison, for instance, spends half a million dollars a year on mussel monitoring.

We can't hope to get rid of zebra mussels. The best we can do is keep their population in balance so that they'll do it themselves by eating up their natural food supply. Many methods have been advanced for curbing them: sending divers to scrape boat bottoms, attempting to introduce premature spawning, heat treatment, the use of chemicals. To all these methods there is a downside. The mussels are so new to the Great Lakes that we don't yet know enough about

them to understand how effective or how dangerous human interference can be.

Certainly there will be far-reaching changes in the ecosystems of the Great Lakes. With their eating habits, the mussels short-circuit the food web. Each mussel filters about a litre of protoplasm every day. Parts of Lake Erie are showing the effect of this; the clarity of the once murky waters of the western basin has increased by 80 percent. That's a boon for water feeders and aquatic plants but not for the pickerel, which can't stand sunlight. The mussels can also be used to detect excess pollution just as a canary can detect deadly gases in a mine. When the water isn't pure, they close their shells. Electrodes attached to some shells can trigger an early warning system. Another benefit is to the diving ducks, a species that preys on zebra mussels. At Point Pelee, the population of two handsome species—the greater and lesser scaup—has increased from one hundred to twenty thousand.

But the bonuses are tiny. They cannot outweigh the costs and the trouble of dealing with these and other intruders. Attempts to have ocean ships drop their water ballast before entering the system have been partially successful. We will have to learn to live with the zebra mussel just as we learned to live with the sea lamprey. The price cannot now be calculated, but the bill must be paid. It is one of those unseen charges that cannot be determined in advance but that inevitably occur when mankind tries to fiddle with the natural order. In the Great Lakes ecosystem, every change represents a trade-off. To rephrase an old cliché, we have found that we cannot eat our lake trout and have them too.

The people's lakes

For at least two centuries, men, women, and toddlers have disported themselves in the waters and on the sands of the great inland seas.

The diving competition was a highlight of the Canadian National Exhibition in 1935. The ladies on the right were known as bathing beauties back in the 1920s when this photo was taken at Edgewater Beach, Chicago. They're all members of The Earl Carol's Vanities Chorus.

160

Back in 1901 no one had designed a fishing costume for proper young Toronto ladies. But there were more fish.

In 1910, iceboat sailing on Toronto Bay had reached its zenith. Iceboats are passé today, but the elite still indulge in sailing regattas as they did in Chicago (LEFT) back in 1905.

A family outing on Georgian Bay in the days before television and speedboats. This is the extended France family posing for a snapshot during an annual outing at Minnicognashene.
RIGHT: *Kite flying at Grand Haven on Lake Michigan.*

*On Wasaga Beach, the most popular
(and most crowded) of the lake
playgrounds, small-fry make pies of
sand as they always have.*

*Sailboats of every size and design
roam the windswept thirty
thousand islands of Georgian Bay.*

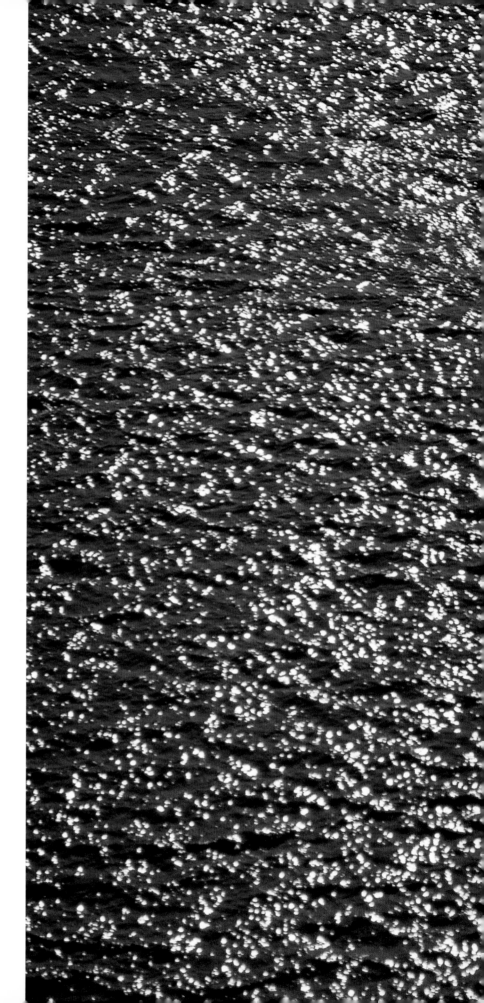

The water slide at Crystal Beach, Michigan (TOP), is just steep enough but not too steep for all but the timid. Wasaga Beach, Georgian Bay (BOTTOM), is so jammed with sweating humanity that it's sometimes difficult to find the lake. In Chicago (RIGHT), fishermen don't need to hike or paddle into the wilderness. They can throw their lines from one of the city's docks.

Chicago's string of waterfront parks separates the skyscraper jungle from the lake.

CHAPTER NINE

HOW MUCH IS A VIEW WORTH?

THE GLORY OF EVERY CITY SITUATED ON ONE OF THE INLAND SEAS OUGHT TO BE ITS lakefront. I say "ought to be" because in instance after instance the aesthetic qualities have been shoved aside in the interests of commerce. In the nineteenth century, the docks, grain elevators, and factories that still mar most shorelines were held to be far more important than such ephemeral considerations as an uninterrupted view of sparkling waters or morning mists. Duluth's cluttered shoreline, for instance, consists of fifty dreary miles of docks. Cleveland's two tiny waterfront parks, one on each side of town, are unused, neglected, and hard to find. As far as public access is concerned, the rest is wasteland—a narrow, useless strip of land on the edge of the freeway. Only recently have some of the lake cities—my own Toronto is a good example—tried to redress the balance.

There is, of course, one magnificent exception. Chicago, in 1836, did what no other city in the world has since done. It preserved twenty miles of shoreline for the use of all—"probably the most stunning park system in the world," to quote its historian, Lois Wille. The city would "give its most priceless land, its infinitely valuable shoreline to its people. The lake front would be dedicated to pleasure and beauty, not to commerce and industry."

I first saw Chicago in the spring of 1948, having by then endured Toronto for the best part of a year. It was a bit of a culture shock, albeit a welcome one. I felt I had been released temporarily from prison. To me, at that time, Chicago was everything Toronto was not. The largest American city on the lakes seemed to have little in common with the largest Canadian city on the same waters.

The contrast between the two has narrowed since then. In those days, Chicago was the immigrant city of North America, a crazy quilt of neighbour-hoods that at one time had made it the largest Lutheran city in the world, the second-largest Polish, Bohemian, and Ukrainian city, and the third-largest Swedish and Jewish city in the world. Toronto was a set of uptight villages of white Anglo-Saxon Protestants run not by boisterous Southern Irish, as Chicago was, but by dour men of Ulster who controlled the city council and made the Orangemen's Day parade the biggest event in town. It was still very much a colonial city, loyal to King and Empire. The biggest hotel was Royal; so were the conservatory of music, the museum, the agricultural fair, and the leading bank. Even the animal hospital was royal. Chicago, by contrast, had recently enjoyed a mayor, "Big Bill" Thompson, who won an election by threatening to punch King George V in the nose if he should ever visit the Windy City.

Things have changed since those days. Chicago is no longer "hog butcher to the world"; Toronto is no longer "Hogtown." Chicago has mellowed;

Toronto, thanks to a totally different population mix, has become one of the liveliest cities on the continent. The new Torontonians belong to one hundred different ethnic groups, and they want the lake back.

In the end they may get what Chicago already has and is fighting to keep. In 1834 that metropolis was a village of no more than three thousand when an all-male town meeting, concerned that the historic site of Fort Dearborn would shortly be given over to industry, resolved that the land fronting on Lake Michigan "shall be preserved in all time to come for a public square accessible at all times to the citizens." This was bold talk, but Chicago was already a bold community imbued with all the optimism that distinguished those early pilgrims who took part in the western odyssey.

Two years later, the three commissioners charged with overseeing a new canal decided not to sell a valuable strip of lake frontage. On the edge of their map they wrote: "Public Ground—A Common to Remain Forever Open, Clear, and Free of any buildings or other obstruction whatever."

It was those words that set the tone for the establishment of the remarkable string of lakeshore parks that are Chicago's glory. Many public figures have been involved in the fight to preserve the city's window on its lake, including the tough-minded department store tycoon Aaron Montgomery, who fought successfully for an open lakefront; Daniel Burnham, who helped create the "White City" on the lake—the World's Columbian Exposition of 1893—and who told Chicago's business leaders that "beauty has always paid better than any other commodity"; and Frederick Law Olmsted, the creator of New York's Central Park, who designed the belt of parks along the Chicago waterfront and the broad green runway that connects them.

Not even the great fire of 1871 deterred Chicago from its beautification plan. Indeed, it spurred it on. Somehow the parks commissioners succeeded in converting nearly two thousand acres of meadow, wasteland, and marsh into eight big parks, twenty-nine smaller ones, and thirty-five miles of open lakeshore. It cost twenty-four million dollars, an unbelievable sum in those days.

All this time Toronto was talking big about its waterfront and acting small. In those Calvinist years, commercial considerations outweighed all others. As early as 1818, when Chicago was only a fort in the mud at the end of Lake Michigan, the province of Upper Canada patented thirty downtown acres to five prominent citizens "to hold the same for the use and benefits of the inhabitants." Brave words, but hollow ones. Nothing happened. In the 1840s a citizens' petition urged that a public promenade be built on the reserve. It failed. In 1852

To me, Chicago was everything Toronto was not — a high-wide-and-handsome metropolis, boldly facing Lake Michigan, in sharp contrast to the narrow, uptight community that had turned its back on Lake Ontario.

PREVIOUS PAGES: In the shadow of Chicago's downtown high-rises, the protected lakeshore becomes a magnet for thousands besides providing an unobstructed view of Michigan's waters for the people who gaze out of the office buildings.

the city council tried to get some Crown land to ensure public control of the shoreline, and the City Surveyor laid out on paper a series of "pleasure drives, walks, and shrubbery for the recreation of the citizens." But puritan ideas prevailed. One colonial official declared that the plan was "altogether too ornamental." The city sold off the strip to commercial enterprises.

The idea of an esplanade—a tree-shaded boulevard to follow the contours of the waterfront—was mooted as early as 1837. Nothing came of that until railway fever gripped the province more than a decade later. Several plans were then advanced, all seeking to accommodate the railways. One widely heralded scheme suggested a public walk along the top of the bank, linked by sloping bridges to the rail yards built on filled land below. The *Globe* called it "magnificent," pointing out that the city would have a boulevard "unparalleled in America for extent and beauty of position." An equally ambitious proposal suggested a Front Street terrace, 120 feet wide, separating the railway lands below with a parapet and rows of trees.

None of these proposals was accepted. Instead, a narrow-minded city opted for a narrow esplanade lined with warehouses to the north and railway tracks to the south. The Grand Trunk Railway was behind that scheme and used its clout to force the council to cave in; otherwise, it said, it would move its operations north of the city.

In the years that followed the city surrendered almost all control over public access to the lake. The railways, notably the Canadian Pacific, called the tune. They owned half the core waterfront. When the Citizens' Association commissioned a survey urging a new track elevation by way of a viaduct, together with a twenty-six-acre waterfront park "for the general use of the public," the CPR blocked it on the basis of cost. The company got what it wanted when it was granted a massive rail yard stretching a mile and a half from Yonge Street to Bathurst Street in the very heart of the business district. For more than a century this vast complex has acted as a barrier between the city and the lake.

Again and again the story of Toronto's waterfront was one of grandiose plans never implemented. In 1912 the Toronto Harbour Commissioners gained jurisdiction over 83 percent of the lakefront and came up with a new nineteen-million-dollar plan, hailed by the press as far-sighted and exciting. Toronto, the *Mail and Empire* declared, would achieve status "among the great cities of the world."

Alas, very little was done. Ashbridge's Bay, a swampy wetland to the east of the city, was filled in, but the main recommendations—a three-mile recreation strip, a seawall, a protected waterway, a sylvan boulevard, parkland—were ignored. Part of the plan had been to link the crescent of islands guarding Toronto Bay, but that too was abandoned. To the west, the waterfront would be the site of "the most ideal and comprehensive playground and pleasure resort that a large city could desire." What the city finally got, a decade later, was the Sunnyside amusement area, a tawdry complex of carnival rides and hot-dog stands. As a small boy visiting Toronto from the Yukon, I thought it the best thing about the city; later, as a resident, I was happy to see it demolished. This area, at last, has become parkland.

In a sense, Toronto and Chicago are mirror images of the same problem. Since I first visited Chicago, its citizens have been involved in a long struggle to preserve what they have. At the same time Toronto has been engaged in the opposite struggle—to create what it has never had.

As Lois Wille has pointed out, every one of the disastrous developments that have severely damaged Chicago's park system has been the result of government action. "It wasn't big business and cold commerce that robbed the people of their land, but the people's government, acting in the name of expediency."

Part of the blame can be laid to the politicization of the city's parks through the interference of Chicago's notorious ward bosses, labour leaders loyal to city hall, real estate dealers, and investment brokers. Chicago civic groups have fought hard to preserve the lakefront but not always successfully. "It was government action that paved the lawns into highways, built a convention hall, an airport and two filtration plants on the shore, leased park land to the Army and to private clubs, grew slipshod in park maintenance, pushed for a sports stadium on the lakefront and an airport in the waters." The greensward has now been paved for ten blocks along Lakeshore Drive. "You can have too much green grass," was the remarkable riposte of James Gately, a longtime park district president, when protesters tried (eventually successfully) to stop the building of a gargantuan music bowl on the shore.

Meanwhile, Toronto has struggled to come to terms with its waterfront. In 1943, a highly praised master plan tried to cope with a lake cut off from the city by acres of railway lands built on fill. By this time the automobile was replacing the railways as the villain of the piece. The 1943 plan proposed the building of a new superhighway along the lake; most people applauded, then wished they hadn't. It led, a little more than a decade later, to the construction of the Gardiner Expressway, which the social critic Robert Fulford has called "the largest piece of urban furniture in Toronto." A multilane strip of concrete raised on stilts, it obscures the lake and represents "the most intractable problem facing

In a sense, Toronto and Chicago are mirror images of the same problem. Chicago's citizens have been involved in a long struggle to preserve what they have. At the same time, Toronto has been engaged in the opposite struggle—to create what it has never had.

PREVIOUS PAGES: **The view from the Toronto islands looking toward the city is unobstructed. But the reverse view across the lake from the business section is blocked by industrial buildings, rail yards, and a superhighway.**

those who want to bring life to the waterfront." One solution would be to bury the central part of the superhighway in an underground tunnel, but again, as always, the question of cost stands in the way. What, after all, is a view worth? As Buckminster Fuller declared in 1968, "when moving around in the downtown, one is totally unaware that Toronto is a waterfront, not a prairie, city."

Nevertheless, even as Fuller was making that pronouncement, the city fathers of Toronto, unlike their contemporaries in Chicago, were listening to a public that, more and more, was demanding a new look. A new metropolitan plan, launched in 1967, asserted that future development must take place "in an orderly, coordinated, and imaginative manner" with significant benefits to be conferred on the public realm.

That prospect was given a considerable boost in 1970 when, as an election ploy, the federal government presented Toronto with a forty-acre piece of lakefront in the central core. In one sense, Harbourfront (as it is officially called) has been wildly successful. Its marinas, restaurants, art galleries, and theatres have brought new life to the lakeshore. Each year three million people beat a cluttered path to its door through the labyrinth of tunnels, cross streets, and expressway ramps that still bar the way to the lake. But Harbourfront had to be paid for—and that was the rub. The erection of a hotel and several apartment buildings on the property stuck in the craw of most citizens. Like the Gardiner, they impede an unrestricted view of the water.

But attitudes have been changing. As in Chicago, a militant public cannot be ignored forever. Early in the 1960s, the city proposed to construct the Gardiner Expressway directly through the site of old Fort York, whose history goes back to the War of 1812. Here was irony. The very "improvements" made to the waterfront over the years were being used by the expressway's proponents to support this vandalism. The fort was originally built on a strategic property overlooking the lake. Since that time tonnes of fill had changed the contours of the shoreline so greatly that the fort was now half a mile from the water. Fred Gardiner, the Supermayor for whom the expressway would be named, urged that the fort be moved to a more convenient location. After all, didn't it belong on the water? As I wrote at the time, that would be akin to moving the Plains of Abraham.

The city bowed to public pressure, and the fort remained where it had always been but ringed, alas, by concrete roadways. Yet those who find their way to it are today treated to a visual lesson in history. From here it is possible to picture how Toronto has changed since the waters of the lake lapped at the bottom of the strategic cliff on which Fort York was built.

The general concern over the lakefront peaked in 1988, when the federal government assigned the former "tiny, perfect mayor," David Crombie, to chair the Royal Commission on the Future of the Toronto Waterfront. In 1992, this body became the Waterfront Regeneration Trust, with Crombie at its head.

Transportation has always been the enemy of the environment. And so we Torontonians continue to suffer the Gardiner at the expense of the vistas it helps conceal—and will until it is removed or buried. The perceptive travel writer Jan Morris has called our town "one of the most highly disciplined and tightly organized cities of the Western world." I'm not sure whether she meant that as a knock or a boost. She could not say that about Chicago, certainly, and since these words were written in 1984 they are, I think, less applicable today.

Both these big lake cities have undergone startling transformations. Successive waves of immigrants have changed their character. The writer Richard Lindberg has called Chicago "the most ethnically and culturally diverse of all American cities." The same phrase, in Canada, applies to Toronto.

Consider these figures: of the two hundred thousand newcomers who chose Toronto as their home between 1990 and 1992, two out of five could not speak either of the two official languages. Few were WASPs. Seventy percent came from Asia, Africa, Central and South America, and the Caribbean. My town is no longer the uptight city I knew after the war. The figures suggest that by 2001 more than half the metropolitan population will be members of a racial minority. And that, I think, has led to a new tolerance—and also new attitudes about what a lake city should be.

I note these changes as I drive south from my country home down the valley of the Humber River to enter the city through its western front door at Humber Bay. Here, if I take the Lake Shore Boulevard, I experience a sense of déjà vu, for this seven-mile stretch of parkland from the river's mouth past the Exhibition grounds is reminiscent of the Chicago waterfront. Here you can see the early beginnings of a lakefront resurrection. Sunnyside is only a memory. A different kind of amusement area—Ontario Place—the kind envisaged by early planners, with lagoons, shade trees, pathways, sand hillocks beside restaurants and theatres, has taken its place across from Exhibition Park.

It is a joy to travel along the lake through the parkland, with the maples swaying in the breeze, the dew still on the grass, and the waters of Lake Ontario lapping at the shoreline.

But I must confess that, when I'm in a hurry (as I usually am), I opt for Fred Gardiner's concrete monstrosity.

Both these big lake cities have undergone startling transformations. Successive waves of immigrants have changed their character. Is this one of the factors that has given Toronto its reputation as the most wide-open city on the continent?

An album of ethnic diversity

TORONTO'S ASTONISHING TRANSFORMATION

Successive waves of immigrants have changed the faces of the Great Lakes communities, none more so than that of Toronto. The all-British community that once called itself York now listens to the babel of a hundred tongues.

These contrasting photographs tell the story. No one could confuse these men, taking their ease on the benches of today's Little Italy, with the all-British contingent shown arriving in Toronto in 1908.

Newcomers cluster together in Toronto's ethnic areas. Gerrard Street East (BELOW LEFT) is a blaze of East Indian colour. So is the Portuguese enclave across town, where people enjoy their own festivals (BELOW RIGHT) and the houses are painted in rainbow hues.

Since the arrival of the first Jewish immigrants more than a century ago, Kensington Market, off Spadina Avenue, has been a centre for newcomers, like these turn-of-the-century street musicians (RIGHT).

Well over half a century ago, these children of various backgrounds were photographed mingling in the streets of Toronto.

The harsh laws that restricted an Oriental population are long gone. As a result, Toronto has not one but four Chinatowns.

CHICAGO: THE TRADITIONAL MELTING POT

Long before Toronto put out the welcome mat, Chicago was
a haven for a polyglot mix of newcomers, many of whom
arrived not from Europe but from the American South.

*The young men in the picture on the left, celebrating Easter morning on
Chicago's South Side in April 1941, belong to the children of black immigrants who
had moved up the Mississippi in earlier days, bringing with them
the jazz culture for which the city became known. In its turn, a later wave of
Mexicans, like the young basketball player shown here, has followed the blacks.*

As in Toronto, street signs in Chicago are sometimes bilingual. But the ethnic mix is different. In spite of a thriving Chinatown, there are fewer Orientals but far more Southern Irish and Poles per capita. The last arrived before the turn of the century, like the heavily burdened family on the right.

There are sections of Chicago where you won't see a white face for blocks—even in the Chinese restaurants. Chicago has many faces—from the elaborately coiffured African-American woman on the left to the parking attendant in Greek Town, above.

CHAPTER TEN

THE FIGHT TO SAVE THE INLAND SEAS

Wasaga Beach (ABOVE) suffered from a different kind of pollution for years when automobiles used it as a parking lot. Happily, that's no longer allowed. In 1917, artists, writers, poets, performers, and conservationists mounted an ambitious pageant on the Indiana Dunes (OPPOSITE) in an attempt to have the entire area made into a national park. They were ahead of their time, but the fight went on.

DURING MY LIFETIME I HAVE WITNESSED A REMARKABLE CHANGE OF ATTITUDE toward the environment. It has its roots in the nineteenth century when the whole concept of public parks for the people began to make itself felt. Effective though they often were, these movements were generally the work of a minority of intellectuals. It was not until the 1960s, when a new generation was heard from, that a two-pronged effort to protect our national heritage and to save us from industrial pollution began to gather momentum. It still has a long way to go.

With close to thirty-five million people living along their shores, it is not surprising that the Great Lakes bear little resemblance to the great sheets of fresh water that awed the first Europeans. It is as if some demonic being had drained them all dry and replaced the water with a totally foreign liquid, infested with strange flora and fauna and befouled by no fewer than 362 contaminants, a third of which can have acute or toxic effects on life.

Vicki Keith, the twenty-nine-year-old marathon swimmer, got more than a whiff of this when she crossed Lake Ontario in August 1990. The pollution she encountered devastated her. After she swam through a "toilet bowl current" of raw sewage, her ears hurt and she vomited continually. Dead seagulls floated in her path as she made her way from the mouth of the Niagara to the Leslie Street spit in Toronto. She emerged with a layer of scum on her bathing suit and goggles. "I have never seen anything so disgusting," she declared. In the words of Dr. Gary Sprules, a University of Toronto biologist, "there is nothing natural about the lake. It is almost entirely artificial."

Only in recent decades have we begun to care about the environment in which we live. That word in its current meaning had scarcely entered the lexicon before the protest movements of the sixties. About the same time, another strange word, "ecology"—the science of the relationship between organisms and the environment—also became part of the popular argot.

A citizens' movement sprang up demanding that the waters be cleared of pollution and the beaches and forests preserved for the public good. I doubt that it would have been as effective as it has been without the presence of television cameras to record the protest marches and rallies. Television thrives on

Bethlehem Steel created one of the two great industrial complexes that have gobbled up so much of the unique Indiana Dunes.

controversy, as everybody from the First Nations to the animal rights movement has learned. Thus, it isn't surprising that not until the 1960s was the general public aware that the Great Lakes, especially Erie, were in trouble.

It was said that Lake Erie was dying—a "North American Dead Sea," to quote one catchphrase. The real truth was that the lake wasn't dead at all; it was too much alive for its own good. Quantities of sewage, industrial waste, and farm runoffs were enriching its waters to the point where the resultant algal bloom was taking over. Erie was becoming "a monster that stinks and exudes thick mats of green, decomposing slime" in the description of William Ashworth, author of *The Late, Great Lakes.*

The enemy was phosphate, a major farm fertilizer found also in the new miracle detergents once promoted to housewives as the answer to soap. For years the major detergent manufacturers fought a hard but eventually losing battle to retain phosphorus in their products. A consumer revolt, with government backing, finally won out. One is reminded of the long struggle by the tobacco manufacturers to persuade the public that nicotine doesn't cause cancer. In Canada, the very housewives the detergent companies were wooing became some of their chief opponents. "Remember please, we care about our comforts—but we care more about our children and their future in our civilization," one women's rally proclaimed.

As a result, the amount of phosphates in detergents has been reduced to a minuscule amount and the lakes are relatively free of algal bloom. The campaign is, as Russell Train of the U.S. Environmental Protection Agency declared, "one of the greatest success stories in American history." No doubt it has been. But the

problem is much broader. The postwar chemical revolution that has seen everything from solvents to pesticides indiscriminately dumped into the lakes is going
to cost the taxpayers of both countries an eventual hundred billion dollars.

We are going to have to pay the price because the health of the human
species is at stake. Some three hundred chemicals pollute the Great Lakes. We
are now beginning to understand that these chemicals cannot be washed away
or diluted. It was once thought that they would be so widely dispersed and
broken down that they would not cause a problem. We have learned that they
persist for years and are carried through the ecosystem, ending up so far from
the original source that control is difficult.

The results can be seen in the offspring of some fifteen species of wildlife
in thinner shells, cleft palates, club feet, and crossed bills. As a result of DDT, for
instance, the eggs of the osprey are so thin that few young are hatched and the
species is threatened with extinction. A troubling study of pulp waste in Jackfish
Channel on Lake Superior showed that some chemical in the waste is disrupting
sexual development of male whitefish. In fact, it's hard to tell the sex of some of
these fish. Dr. Theo Colborn of the World Wildlife Fund now says "it's very hard
to find a male fish that reaches full sexual maturation in the Great Lakes."

The implications for humans are even more disturbing. A four-year human
health study in Detroit has charted the toxic effects of chemicals on the children
of mothers who regularly ate contaminated fish in the 1970s. The results suggest
that the memory and learning ability of these children have been adversely
affected. As Dr. Colborn has said, the Great Lakes are "a very, very sick system."

More recently the public has been made aware that the very air is itself a major contributor to water pollution. An investigation by the *Toronto Star* in October 1995 revealed that 85 percent of the toxic chemicals polluting the Canadian shore of Lake Ontario (fifteen million kilograms) is the result of contaminated air from automobile, steel, pharmaceutical, and commercial printing plants, an airport, and a wallpaper manufacturer. Who would have thought that wallpaper could befoul the water we drink? But the figures reveal that the Brampton company that makes it ranks third on the list of the ten worst polluters around the lake as a result of the chemical solvents that escape from wallpaper inks during the oven-drying process.

Like the housewives who put their children's futures ahead of easier washing methods, consumers on both sides of the border are going to have to exchange some creature comforts for cleaner lake water. For every scientific and technological advance, we have paid a price. We wanted a ship canal to link the lakes; we got alewives and zebra mussels. We wanted a "whiter than white" laundry product; we got algal bloom. We wanted plastic toys, plastic dishes, plastic everything; we got Love Canal.

Industry will not act to save the lakes, nor will governments, unless pushed and prodded. It is the people's movements that have always done the pushing—the consumer advocates, the environmentalists, the amateur ecologists, the "nuts" and radicals who wave signs and launch boycotts. If the lakes are cleaner today it is because the public has demanded it, dragging industry kicking and screaming into the twentieth century.

If some of the land is finally being set aside as wilderness areas it is because the public has insisted. The movement is comparatively young. Not until recently have the forests and shorelines, the dunes, the beaches, and the wetlands that border the lakes been thought of as priceless assets to be retained for future generations.

Perhaps the greatest example of a popular ecological movement intent on saving a chunk of wilderness is the fifty-year-long battle to preserve a section of the Indiana Dunes on Lake Michigan. The dunes, a forty-mile strip of shifting sand, forest, bog, slough, shallow lakes, and stormy beach, are about an hour's drive from Chicago's Loop. They have been called the birthplace of North American ecology. From the standpoint of vegetation they are the most complex sand dunes in the world, for here can be seen the physical evidence of Lake Michigan's shrinkage during the various stages of the glacial runoff. A series of sandswept ridges represents the ancient shorelines. The highest ridge is a beach line that goes back twelve thousand years. Thus, as you climb up these ridges from today's lakeshore, you are actually walking back up the steps of time. Here, in this classic laboratory of ecological succession, are to be found a variety of environments: northern plant species, such as tamarack and Arctic bearberry; many southern species, such as tulip tree, black gum, and sassafras; such western prairie types as meadow grass and cacti; and eastern woodland plants, such as sugar maples, beech, and trillium.

It was this rich mixture of many elements that captured the imagination of the Chicago social reformers, artists, ecologists, poets, novelists, and campers who joined in the long battle to save the dunes. As Herbert Read, the author and critic, wrote, the dunes' significance was "not vested in one or two of its natural features, but in its combination and diversity of features. . . . It is the *totality* that is significant."

This was a landmark campaign. One of its founders, Henry Chandler Cowles, has been called the father of modern ecology. While pursuing a doctorate at the University of Chicago in the late 1890s, Cowles used the dunes as a living laboratory and gained an international reputation as a pioneer in the field of plant ecology and a strong leader in the fight to preserve this unusual strip of lakefront.

The dunes probably inspired more eloquence than any other part of the North American environment, with the exception of Niagara Falls. After all, many of the dunes advocates were writers and poets. It was "the sacred centre of the religion of democracy," "the vast garden of mid-America," "a special place apart," a "veritable floral melting pot." The dunes fostered an incredible literature—literally hundreds of items from novels and poems to speeches—as well as pageants, paintings, sculpture, etchings, and films: an educational campaign of immense significance.

The idea that certain parts of the wilderness should be set aside for the future was too new in 1906 to prevent U.S. Steel from erecting its Gary Works spang in the heart of the Lake County Dunes, thus destroying that section forever. Only the slow emergence of a national conservation ethic eventually saved those fragments of the dunes that are still preserved.

In 1916 the dunes movement tried to get Congress to establish a national Indiana Dunes park. That suggestion was considered far too radical. Forty years would pass and much of the dunes environment would be destroyed by the building of another steel plant before the matter was brought up again at the federal level. Meanwhile, in 1923, the Save the Dunes movement managed to have a two-thousand-acre segment set aside as a state park. It was a small but remarkable victory that ran counter to the generally

The postwar chemical revolution that has seen everything from solvents to pesticides dumped into the lakes is going to cost the taxpayers of both countries an eventual hundred billion dollars.

199

accepted view that progress should be measured solely in economic and industrial terms.

Those who fought for the dunes and arranged parades and pageants to celebrate their variety had no vested interest, only their childhood memories of playing in what one of them has called "the sacred sands." Until it attracted the populist Senator Paul Douglas to the cause in 1958, the movement was essentially amateur. Douglas fought hard for a national rather than a state park to preserve what was left of the dunes. The result was the eleven-thousand-acre Indiana Dunes National Lakeshore, a collection of those jigsaw-puzzle pieces of land that had not been given over to steel mills, highways, rail lines, shopping centres, housing developments, and a new deep-water port. Without the long struggle, the dunes would have been entirely swallowed by development. Nor, without the pioneering work and experience of the Save the Dunes movement, could a similar coalition of environmentalists, labour activists, and antinuclear groups have stopped the completion of a nuclear reactor on the dunes. That was the first time a nuclear project under construction was abandoned because of public protest.

The long campaign for the dunes added to the growing awareness that the wilderness was not an enemy to be destroyed but an asset to be preserved. The conservation movement did not gather steam, however, until the 1950s, when the camping craze hit North America. The province of Ontario, which has shores on four of the five Great Lakes, was one government that began to find itself under pressure not only from the conservationists but also from ordinary citizens who wanted a place to pitch a tent.

The figures are astonishing. In 1954, Ontario had only eight public parks, five of them on the Great Lakes. By 1989 that total had zoomed to a staggering 261. Suddenly people were demanding more of the lakes for themselves—groups such as the Association for the Preservation of East Erie Lakefront, which mounted a successful public protest against private ownership of lakeside property. The signs that small children carried said it all: "Fences are for cattle, not people."

But what *are* parks for? Should they be available to everybody for recreational activities? Should they be equipped with benches, camping areas, barbecue pits, changing rooms, and cottages? Should some areas be set aside to preserve the wilderness untouched? Or is the preservation of the wilderness incompatible with the tourist trade? The Federation of Ontario Naturalists, as early as 1961, declared that this was so: "The preservation of an area in its natural state is, generally speaking, incompatible with recreational use." That year, thanks to the preservationists, Ontario set aside thirty-five wilderness

areas, all but ten selected as nature reserves. Most bordered on the Great Lakes.

The first and largest, Pukaskwa, on the rugged north shore of Superior, was later transferred to the federal government and became a national park. Its chief purpose is preservation; 90 percent of its area has been zoned "wilderness," free of motorized intrusion, its quota of visitors—mainly backpackers—carefully rationed. But there is also another smaller area zoned for outdoor recreation where a full range of visitor uses and related facilities are available.

Pukaskwa, in short, has managed to cater to both the preservationists and the campers. One is reminded of the long struggle that took place between the cottagers who leased property at Rondeau Provincial Park on Lake Erie and those who wanted to preserve the superb Carolinian forest (rare to our northern clime) at the point of the peninsula without the incursions of holidayers.

The solution was worthy of a Solomon. In the end the government simply split the park in two.

Happily, the photograph above of two hunters triumphantly posing with their kill of swans is now outmoded. After a long struggle between conservationists and gun owners, hunting has finally been banned in Point Pelee National Park. It was always an anomaly.

Three parks by the shore

The postwar camping craze started it all. In 1954 Ontario had only eight public parks—five on the lakes. Today there are 261 in that province alone.

PUKASKWA IN THE SUMMER

The first and largest of the new wilderness areas, it is designed to protect the boreal forest of the Shield and the rugged coastline of Lake Superior.

Now a national park with 90 percent designated as wilderness area and free of motorized intrusion, Pukaskwa offers white-water adventure, trout fishing, canoeing, and cross-country skiing.

ISLE ROYALE
IN THE FALL

*Set like a jewel in the
westerly waters of Lake Superior,
it is the most inaccessible
national park in the continental
United States. And there isn't a
single public road on the island!*

*Copper miners worked the island
in three great successive waves,
then departed for good. It is now
part of the United States National
Wilderness Preservation System
and is also an International
Biosphere Reserve, in recognition
of its unique ecosystem.*

The island is not easy to get at. Boats from the mainland are often thrown off schedule by the weather and there is no place for cars. Nonetheless canoeists and hikers find it a paradise and many return year after year from mid-May to mid-October when the park is open.

FATHOM FIVE PARK IN WINTER

Canada's first national marine park encompasses an unspoiled archipelago of nineteen islands.

The lighthouse at Big Tub marks the entrance to the park, which is situated at Burnt Point on the tip of the Bruce Peninsula near Tobermory. Here the Niagara Escarpment disappears under the water to re-emerge as a series of rocky islands, one of which, Middle Island, can be seen in the distance in the photograph on the right.

210

Gales blowing off Lake Huron encase the park in a mantle of snow and ice.
These treacherous waters claimed at least twenty-one sail and steam vessels in the mid-19th and early 20th centuries

Most of the park is under water and has become a favourite spot for scuba divers. At the tip of the Bruce Peninsula, the ancient limestone, grooved and pitted by the moving glacier, dips under the surface to re-emerge as islands in Lake Huron.

CHAPTER ELEVEN

MY LOVE AFFAIR WITH POINT PELEE

ABOVE: Captured in the photographer's lens during the great spring warbler migration, a yellow warbler feeds among the catkins of a hop tree.
PREVIOUS PAGES: The birds are out at dawn and so are the birders at Pelee, forsaking their breakfasts to identify their quarry in the beams of the rising sun.

CONSIDER THE ASTONISHING PROLIFERATION OF NEW PARKS THAT LIE ALONG THE travelled shores of the five Great Lakes! A little more than a century ago there were none. Now, by my count, there are one hundred and twenty—with public space reserved for many more on both sides of the border. They come in all shapes and sizes—state parks, federal parks, national parks, provincial parks. What a distance we have travelled since that July day in 1885 when the State of New York opened its Niagara Falls Reservation! It was a landmark undertaking, for it established the novel concept that private property could be expropriated for purely aesthetic reasons.

Today there are parks for everyone. They stretch from Presqu'ile Point, on the northeastern shore of Lake Ontario, to Isle Royale in the old copper country at the far end of Superior. There are parks where skin divers can explore old shipwrecks (Fathom Five) and parks where orchid lovers can feast their eyes on more than forty species (Bruce Peninsula). There are parks for history buffs, for canoeists, for young families, for hikers, even for butterfly fanciers. There are hard-to-reach parks, such as Quetico, the inaccessible wilderness area beyond Superior, and easy-to-reach parks, such as Wasaga Beach, the sunbather's paradise on Georgian Bay.

Everybody has a favourite park and I have mine. In the spring, Point Pelee National Park on Lake Erie is as close to paradise as I hope to get. In mid-March when the Toronto winter seems interminable, it bedevils my sleep. Will May never come? As the last blizzards swirl, visions sustain me—visions of a hardwood forest carpeted in bellwort, spring beauty, and sweet cicely; of the emerging foliage dappled with the butterfly tints of wood warblers; of the vast marsh, croaking and buzzing with redwing blackbirds; of the slender sand spit vibrating with thousands of gulls and terns.

I have been visiting Point Pelee each spring for some thirty-five years. Others come in the summer to catch smelt or carp, or in the fall to watch the myriads of monarch butterflies fluttering south. I come for the birds.

Pelee is one of the smallest of our national parks, the ninth in Canada, so designated on May 29, 1918. It was well worth preserving, for it is unique. There is nothing else remotely like it in this country or, indeed, in the world. Because it lies across the forty-second parallel, nearly all of it is in the same latitude as northern California. Its flora is notably un-Canadian. Because two of the great North American flyways overlap it, Pelee has become a Mecca for thousands of birders who pour in from points as distant as Australia, Europe, and Alaska to observe the spring migration.

But Pelee is more than birds. For me it provides the ultimate rite of spring. It is the perfume of the spice bush, the taste of wild asparagus, the buzzing of the nocturnal woodcock, the splash of the carp in the shallow ponds, the sizzle of bacon in the pan, or the aroma of a barbecued steak on an outdoor grill thoughtfully provided for people like me by the park authorities. It is also the camaraderie of utter strangers who rush up to inform you that a blue grosbeak has been spotted near the abandoned orchard, or that a dickcissel has been positively identified on the nature trail. This is more than a national park; it is, for me, a celebration to be looked forward to each year and hungered for when May finally comes.

Pelee is shaped something like an isosceles triangle, its sharpest point jutting out into the shallow waters of the lake. Formed from a ridge of gravel that the glacier deposited across Lake Erie at least ten thousand years ago, it has been, over the eons, covered by sands and pebbles deposited by wind and water. Occasionally this ridge pokes its spine above the surface of the lake, forming a string of islands that act like stepping stones from the south to the north shore and help as guides to the birds on their northern migration. The first land they see is this funnel-shaped promontory with its inviting mix of marsh, forest, field, and bush. Birds that never appear elsewhere in Canada can be found here in May, and sometimes birds that aren't supposed to be here at all. They turn up lost and bewildered, having overshot the lake, and are forced south again in a reverse migration.

At Pelee we rise with the horned larks and make our way down the point to the parking lot near the information centre, where a little train takes us to the tip of the triangle. Before us a slender stretch of sand curves out into the lake, literally covered with the white forms of hundreds of gulls. And here we encounter people from the far corners of the continent—indeed, of the earth—who have come to this little sand spit, driven by a common obsession.

On a Sunday morning at Pelee I talked to one couple who had flown in from Texas to see the birds. That same day I ran into a young man who had driven all the way from Haines Junction in the Yukon for the same purpose. One afternoon I came upon a man who had travelled halfway around the world from Australia to watch the migration and was disconsolate because he thought he'd missed it. His gloom was premature. The warblers were out in record numbers that year—he counted thirty-eight species—making his long journey more than worthwhile. In the old orchard—a relic of a time when this was not a national park—I ran into the legendary Joe Taylor, who was

Pelee is more than birds and more than a national park. For me it provides the ultimate rite of spring—a celebration to be looked forward to each year and hungered for when May finally comes.

217

determined to see more birds than any other human being and was said to have flown his own plane once from Africa to Massachusetts in order to spot a rare gull. And more than once I rubbed shoulders with Norm Chesterfield, the retired Canadian mink farmer who exceeded Joe Taylor's bird count and for some years held title as the world's champion birder. And there, at lunchtime some years ago, was Roger Tory Peterson himself, the man who started the birding fad and whose field guide, published in 1934, sells thirty thousand copies a year in Canada alone.

Standing at the point of the triangle at dawn we can see the great flights struggling in after journeys that can exceed a thousand miles. Exhausted, they pause to rest. Most move on north, but ninety species remain to nest. As the sun rises they begin to sing in a kind of massed choir. The Toronto naturalist John Livingston has written that "nowhere—certainly nowhere in Canada—is there such a memorable morning chorus."

A spur of the Carolinian hardwood forest pokes briefly into "Canada's Deep South," as Pelee has been dubbed. Here flourish species unfamiliar to the rest of Canada—sycamore, hickory, redbud, hoary puccoon—and a profusion of wildflowers, such as the columbine shown below.

Point Pelee is mostly water—a ridge of sand enclosing a core of marsh. Here, among the floating lilies and swamp plants, a dedicated birder can easily spot a short-billed marsh hen or a green heron. Along the shallower ponds within the forest, the exquisite prothonotary warbler makes its nest.

We walk back along the nature trail, hoping to find some confused bird that has come too far—a rarity that we can proudly add to our Life List. But most of the birds are true to form. Pelee is unique in its varied habitats: sand for the sandpipers, old apple trees for the orchard orioles, wetlands for the marsh wrens, sturdy tree trunks for the brown creepers, wood for the woodpeckers.

This is Carolinian country—the last remnants of the great deciduous hardwood forest that once stretched along Erie's shores. Trees, shrubs, and flowers unknown to the rest of Canada thrive in the wooded belt above Pelee's beaches, never more than ten feet higher than the level of the lake. There is sassafras here and shagbark hickory, sycamore and hackberry, all thriving because of the southern latitude and the warming presence of the lake. Pelee enjoys one of the longest frost-free seasons in Canada, which explains, perhaps, why the woods through which I wander are jungles of tangled growth. Vines of poison ivy and grape as thick as a man's wrist entwine the trees, while under my feet the prickly pear cactus flourishes in the sand.

Nine hundred years before Columbus reached America aboriginal peoples lived at Pelee. The bridge of stepping-stone islands made it possible to cross the lake by canoe, providing handy shelter from Erie's violent storms. In those days the peninsula bore little relation to the triangle of marsh, forest, and sand we know today. The early French travellers called it *pelée*, which means "bare" or "bald," because it was devoid of vegetation, at least on the sandy tract along the eastern shore where only cedars flourished. Darryl Stewart, a naturalist writer, has studied the reports of one military engineer who in 1749 portaged across the point by way of the central marsh and has reckoned that the point was probably a mile longer then than it is today.

So Pelee is ever changing. The sand spit at the point takes on a different shape from month to month, from year to year, as the lake encroaches or subsides. The birds extend their range from decade to decade so that species that were rarities half a century ago are common today. The cattle egret, once the close companion of the African water buffalo and totally foreign to North America, seems to be everywhere these days. The orchards the pioneers planted have gone wild; the land they cleared is returning to the forest. Each spring we climb over the great trunks of shallow-rooted giants that have been felled by one of Erie's savage storms. Over the years we watch them rot into the soil, only to discover new saplings rising up from their corpses. Each year the park authorities close some of the trails we have trampled so that the age-old

process of regeneration can continue. On Pelee everything changes, yet nothing changes. We know almost to the week when the redbud will break into blossom, when the Solomon's seal will poke above the mosses, when the first prairie warbler will arrive from Florida and the last tree sparrow will wing off to the tundra. Because of nature's predictable cycles, the Great Lakes seem everlasting and so, in the space of a single lifetime, they are. But no one can predict exactly when the ice will swallow them again, and none can know what new freshwater seas will mark that glacier's passing.

In the great marsh that forms Pelee's soft centre, birders take to canoes to seek out their quarry. The park authorities have built walkways across the swamps, complete with observation towers for photographers and rubbernecks. Egrets and herons soar high above or stand motionless in the water, waiting for their prey. RIGHT: Early on a spring morning, hundreds trek out to the sandspit at Pelee's southern tip to view the gulls, terns, and other shorebirds that congregate in flocks at the far end.

Design and Art Direction: Andrew Smith
Page Composition: Andrew Smith Graphics Inc.
Research: Barbara Sears
Consultant: Elsa Franklin

A GODDARD-ZAXIS PROJECT

ARCHIVAL PICTURE CREDITS

QUETICO PROVINCIAL PARK

SILVER ISLET

HEMLO MINE

ISLE ROYALE NAT'L PARK

PUKASKWA NAT'L PARK

Thunder Bay ●

Grand Portage ●

MINNESOTA

**LAKE
SUPERIOR**

ONTARIO

Duluth ●

Keweenaw Bay

KEWEENAW PENINSULA

Sault Ste Marie ●

*St. Mary's
River*

Blind River ●

Sudbury ●

SOO CANALS

North Channel

French Rive

MACKINAC ISLAND →●

Fort Michilimackinac

MANITOULIN ISLAND

*Georgian
Bay*

Green Bay

FATHOM FIVE NAT'L MARINE PARK

WISCONSIN

Oconto River

**LAKE
HURON**

BRUCE PENINSULA

Saginaw Bay

Milwaukee ●

Muskegon ●

Bay City ●
Saginaw ●

**LAKE
MICHIGAN**

London ●

*St. Clair
River*

Sarnia ●

MICHIGAN

*Lake
St. Clair*

Detroit ●

ILLINOIS

Windsor

**LAKE
ERIE**

Chicago ●

Amherstburg ●

Detroit River

Monroe ●

Illinois River

INDIANA

POINT PELEE NAT'L PARK

Toledo ●

INDIANA DUNES NAT'L LAKESHORE

OHIO

● Cleveland